Tools Not Rules®

Developing **Self-Regulation** for **Improved Student Behavior** in Grades **K–8**

Claudia Bertolone-Smith
and **Marlene Moyer**

Solution Tree | Press

Copyright © 2025 by Solution Tree Press

Materials appearing here are copyrighted. With one exception, all rights are reserved. Readers may reproduce only those pages marked "Reproducible." Otherwise, no part of this book may be reproduced or transmitted in any form or by any means (electronic, photocopying, recording, or otherwise) without prior written permission of the publisher.

555 North Morton Street
Bloomington, IN 47404
800.733.6786 (toll free) / 812.336.7700
FAX: 812.336.7790

email: info@SolutionTree.com
SolutionTree.com

Visit **go.SolutionTree.com/behavior** to download the free reproducibles in this book.

Printed in the United States of America

Library of Congress Cataloging-in-Publication Data

Names: Bertolone-Smith, Claudia, author. | Moyer, Marlene, author.
Title: Tools not rules : developing self-regulation for improved student behavior in grades K-8 / Claudia Bertolone-Smith, Marlene Moyer.
Description: Bloomington, IN : Solution Tree Press, 2025. | Includes bibliographical references and index.
Identifiers: LCCN 2024041417 (print) | LCCN 2024041418 (ebook) | ISBN 9781958590850 (paperback) | ISBN 9781958590867 (ebook)
Subjects: LCSH: Behavior modification. | Self-monitoring. | Classroom management. | Teacher-student relationships.
Classification: LCC LB1060.2 .B48 2025 (print) | LCC LB1060.2 (ebook) | DDC 372.139/3--dc23/eng/20241014
LC record available at https://lccn.loc.gov/2024041417
LC ebook record available at https://lccn.loc.gov/2024041418

Solution Tree
Jeffrey C. Jones, CEO
Edmund M. Ackerman, President

Solution Tree Press
President and Publisher: Douglas M. Rife
Associate Publishers: Todd Brakke and Kendra Slayton
Editorial Director: Laurel Hecker
Art Director: Rian Anderson
Copy Chief: Jessi Finn
Senior Production Editor: Christine Hood
Text and Cover Designer: Kelsey Hoover
Acquisitions Editors: Carol Collins and Hilary Goff
Content Development Specialist: Amy Rubenstein
Associate Editors: Sarah Ludwig and Elijah Oates
Editorial Assistant: Madison Chartier

Acknowledgments

Learning to teach is a journey, and we have gained insight and wisdom from so many amazing mentors along the way. To the master teachers who guided us with patience and love, we are ever grateful. To the students who come through our classroom doors—thank you for your honesty, willingness to try a different path, and the honor to witness you learning more about who you are and what you can do in this world. And to Evy, who started it all by being so stubborn; you have given us an amazing gift—thank you.

Solution Tree Press would like to thank the following reviewers:

Becca Bouchard
Educator
Calgary Academy
Calgary, Alberta

Courtney Burdick
Apprenticeship Mentor Teacher
Spradling Elementary
Fort Smith Public Schools
Fort Smith, Arkansas

John D. Ewald
Educator, Consultant, Presenter, Coach,
　Retired Superintendent,
　Principal, Teacher
Frederick, Maryland

Jenna Fanshier
Sixth-Grade Teacher
Hesston Middle School
Hesston, Kansas

Paige Raney
Chair, Division of Education
Spring Hill College
Mobile, Alabama

Visit **go.SolutionTree.com/behavior** to download the free reproducibles in this book.

Table of Contents

ABOUT THE AUTHORS IX

Introduction 1
    Claudia's Journey 2
    Marlene's Journey 3
    How an Idea Became Tools Not Rules 5
    The Principles of Tools Not Rules 7
    The Tools Not Rules Study 13
    About This Book 14
    Conclusion 16

Chapter 1
Ensuring Honesty Above Anything Else 17
    Honesty as the Foundation 18
    Honest Conversations 21
    Accountability and Honesty 28
    Tools Not Rules for *All* Students, Striving and Advanced 29
    Conclusion 33
    Try This! 33

Chapter 2
Establishing That You Are Not Your Behavior 35

    A Different Approach to Behavior 36
        Actions, Not Labels 37
        Growth Mindset 39
    Positive Student-Teacher Relationships 41
    Students Are Watching 47
    Conclusion 50
    Try This! 50

Chapter 3
Adopting the Tools Not Rules Language 51

    The Meaning of Tools Not Rules Language 52
    The Logic Behind the Three Triads 56
    Common Language in the Classroom and Across the School 57
    The Value of a Predictable Approach 59
    Tools Not Rules Language to Support Schoolwide Programs 61
    Increased Engagement 62
    Conclusion 65
    Try This! 66

Chapter 4
Teaching and Using the Tools Not Rules Language With Students 67

    How to Teach Students the Tools Not Rules Language 68
        How to Set the Stage 71
        The Importance of *We* 72
    Simple Activities for Teaching the Tools Not Rules Language 74
        Sharing Stories 74
        Playing Charades: Are You Shirking, Working,
            or Showboating? 74
        Describing What It Looks Like 74
        Lifting Our Learning 76

Table of Contents

    Modeling Individual Redirection 76
    Modeling Whole-Class Redirection 77
    Setting the Standard 78
A Plan for Rolling Out the Tools Not Rules Language 78
A New Way to Praise Students 83
Individual and Group Assessment 88
    Individual Self-Assessment 88
    Whole-Group Self-Assessment 92
Conclusion 93
Try This! 94

Chapter 5
Changing the Most Challenging Behaviors With the Star Chart 95

Not Your Average Star Chart Story 96
How to Use the Star Chart 99
    Rewards 100
    Privacy 100
    Benefits 101
Support and Reinforcements 103
Simple But Effective 104
Conclusion 105
Try This! 105

Chapter 6
Overcoming Implementation Challenges and Realizing Possibilities 107

Challenges 108
    Getting Started With Tools Not Rules Language 108
    Making Tools Not Rules Words Fit Every Classroom 108
    Setting Parameters for Individual Student Conversations 111
Possibilities 112
    Reducing Teacher Stress 112

Increasing Student Well-Being 114
  Establishing Classroom Routines and Norms 114
 Student Perception Survey 116
  Obtaining Significant Insights 119
  Finding the Meaning Behind Low Scores 120
  Identifying and Attending to Students' Personal Issues 121
 Conclusion 122
 Try This! 122

EPILOGUE: MOVING FORWARD 125
 Confidence in Your Ability to Handle Challenging Behaviors 126
 Courage to Create the Classroom You and Your
  Students Deserve 127
 Community of Educators Who Support Each Other and
  Students in Their Ability to Change 128
 In Closing 129

APPENDIX: THE TOOLS NOT RULES STUDY 131
 Tools Not Rules Study Background 131
 School Demographics and Study Participants 133
 Data Gathering and Analysis 135
  Data Analysis Results 138
  What the Data Tell Us 146
 Conclusion 149

REFERENCES AND RESOURCES 151

INDEX 155

About the Authors

Claudia Bertolone-Smith, PhD, is an associate professor in the School of Education at California State University, Chico. She has been an educator since 1990, with experience teaching first through seventh grade. She has a wide range of educational experiences, from teaching in an urban alternative elementary school focused on involving parents in education, to teaching in a rural environment in schools with diverse populations, varied socioeconomic statuses, and a conservative approach to education. In her current position, Claudia teaches credential program courses in mathematics education.

Claudia is a board member of the California Mathematics Council–North and the Mount Lassen Mathematics Council. She has presented throughout the United States on topics such as development of a positive mathematics identity, units coordination with fractions, mathematics discussion routines, and addressing challenging student behaviors that get in the way of learning.

Claudia received a bachelor's degree in elementary education from the University of Oregon, a master's degree in mathematics education from Walden University, and a doctorate in curriculum, teaching, and learning with a focus on mathematics education from the University of Nevada, Reno.

To learn more about Claudia's work, follow her @toolsnotrules on X. You can find out more about Tools Not Rules at www.toolsnotrules.com or @tools_notrules on Instagram.

Marlene Moyer, MAT, is a seventh-grade English teacher at South Lake Tahoe Middle School in South Lake Tahoe, California. She has taught for more than twenty years in Nevada and California. She was the English department curriculum leader for more than five years and is a mentor teacher.

Marlene was an integral part of her middle school's leadership team that transitioned them to standards-based grading and designed student-friendly critical concepts for student scoring using Robert Marzano's High Reliability Schools model.

Since 2013, Marlene and Claudia have codesigned and copresented at numerous conferences and workshops, including at the CTA Good Teaching Conference in Northern and Southern California, focusing on classroom management strategies that are the basis of Tools Not Rules. They have also presented a family engagement workshop at the Nevada Family Engagement Summit in Las Vegas, Nevada, and a mathematics discourse workshop at the NCTM conference in Denver, Colorado.

Marlene is a member of the California Teachers Association. In 2007, she was awarded Walmart & Sam's Club Local Teacher of the Year; and in 2010, she earned Teacher of the Year from Minden Elementary School in Minden, Nevada.

Marlene earned her bachelor's degree in liberal studies from Santa Clara University in Santa Clara, California. She completed her fifth-year teaching credential and master's degree from Sierra Nevada College in Incline Village, Nevada. Her master's degree study involved best teaching practices for gifted and talented students.

To learn more about Marlene's work, follow her @toolsnotrules on X. You can find out more about Tools Not Rules at www.toolsnotrules.com or @tools_notrules on Instagram.

To book Claudia Bertolone-Smith or Marlene Moyer for professional development, contact pd@SolutionTree.com.

Introduction

> "Tools Not Rules has been instrumental in creating meaningful relationships with my students and class community. I love that it removes shame from conversations and replaces it with empowerment."
>
> **M. Rios**, teacher, grade 6 ELA and ELD, personal communication, October 27, 2023

If you are a classroom teacher, administrator, paraprofessional, or school counselor, you know how difficult it can be to motivate, engage, and encourage students in school when they are stuck, passive, challenging, or feeling silly or unfocused. You also know how much time and energy it takes to create lessons that spark their interest, provide differentiated options, and connect with the most challenging students. Some days, there are small improvements—and they can feel amazing—and other days can feel defeating. The work of educators is more challenging than ever before. We continue to deal with the COVID-19 pandemic academic fallout, social media isolation and polarization, and a rise in mental health issues in young children (Armitage, Collishaw, & Sellers, 2024; Knopf, 2021; Twenge, Haidt, Joiner, & Campbell, 2020). Despite this, those who are called to be teachers persist and continue to grow and stretch their ability to work with students, even amid so much change. If you can relate to this, we hope this book can help!

We are two longtime educators who co-taught grades 5 and 6 together for ten years. Through our frustrations, dedication, and fixation on how to help students succeed, we developed a classroom facilitation approach to working with even the most challenging behaviors. The journey to Tools Not Rules® (TNR) began with trying to maximize learning and minimize behaviors that prevented students from realizing their academic potential. We did not create this method to generate compliance; instead, we created it to help students separate themselves from their behavior. We wanted to shift the belief that academic achievement is something only "smart" students enjoy. We wanted *all* students to succeed, and this requires something different from what we had done in the past. The following sections summarize our personal journeys in building the courage and experience to work with students in a different way.

Claudia's Journey

I always knew I wanted to be a teacher. I was born with the natural ability to work with children. As a teen, I worked for the local recreation department during the summer, took children on outdoor adventures, and helped run summer day camps. I was a lifeguard and taught swim lessons, and when I found myself in college trying to pick a major, teaching elementary school seemed to align best with who I was.

My biggest deficit was that I was born into a family that struggled to manage itself. And by this, I mean that everything was left to chance. We didn't preplan, and we didn't prepare for the difficult circumstances life can bring. Even when we could see a disaster on the horizon (for example, financial issues, housing, health and wellness problems), there wasn't a plan in place to protect us, leaving few choices for how to respond. As a result, not-so-great things happened to us. My parents needing to respond to these types of emergencies left little time for them to notice what their children were doing. Therefore, I was raised without much guidance or consequences. Although there was always love, there was also silence in no one addressing the behaviors my siblings and I exhibited as we grew. This vacuum of not understanding the right approach to discipline was a huge deficit in my ability to teach and manage a classroom. I had to learn the long, arduous, and difficult way—students did not need to like me; they needed my guidance. This journey, fraught with countless trials and errors, taught me many things about myself and about students.

Over the years, I began to trust myself more as I realized connection and correction together showed love and concern. I stopped worrying about being liked as a teacher and started focusing on students learning to know themselves and their strengths. Team teaching with Marlene provided me with a tremendous opportunity to try new things and gauge the results. We held to our belief that *all* students can learn.

This went well for most subjects, but in mathematics, student behaviors erupted. One student would sweep her hair behind her ear and claim, "It isn't possible to solve problems like these!" Some students lost their papers and pencils, and others consistently left to use the restroom. Still others saw mathematics as a time to make sure everyone knew how brilliant they were, took the "mathematics discussion" floor, and let everyone have it: "I know you won't be able to understand this because I worked it out in my head after reading about exponents last night."

We discovered there was a significant correlation between the difficulty of mathematics and the extremity and quantity of behavior. I was intrigued and frustrated because I deeply care about students being able to reason numerically. My son, Evy, was in Marlene's class during this time. Because we were team teaching, I taught Evy mathematics lessons at school. When he had mathematics homework, he would become increasingly agitated and frustrated because he didn't feel like he knew how to do it. I'd ask if I could help, and he would exclaim, "Mom! You don't even know anything about what I have to do! It's so hard, and it doesn't make any sense!" He was fearful, and I know my son. When he felt threatened, he would find a way around it, and this behavior had worked well. He believed he should understand things on the first try; and if he didn't, this meant it was too hard.

When Marlene approached me one day about Evy's behavior during mathematics, I suddenly realized two things: (1) teachers often don't understand the depth of emotion and pain underneath behavior, and (2) children often use behavior to cover up fear, anger, sadness, and other feelings, and to get out of situations that make them uncomfortable. That day, we asked all our students, "What behaviors raise our ability to do mathematics? What behaviors lower our ability?" As a class, we knew that when mathematics got difficult, more of the behaviors would occur.

Marlene's Journey

I didn't start teaching until I was thirty years old. It wasn't that I didn't know what I wanted to do; I just didn't have the energy to do it. As a twenty-year-old liberal studies graduate, I could have taught after leaving school. However, my own mix of childhood challenges and coping skills left me depleted. I just didn't feel like I had anything to give students. I needed more life experience, and I needed to do some of my own healing first.

I grew up in a family with five children. My mother suffered from mental illness and has struggled with this throughout her life. Because of this, I felt ashamed and disconnected. I was constantly trying to hide the elephant in the room. In the classroom, my job was not to learn, but to hide what felt shameful—my mother's mental illness. It was an impossible task, but at the time, it was what I felt I needed to do.

During my childhood, no teachers, principals, or counselors asked the obvious questions: "Are things okay at home? How is it going? How is your mom? How are you?" Even in my family, only one adult relative could address the issues that he saw. As a society, we just weren't there yet, or I, at least, had not met the adults who could help.

So as Claudia and I began developing the Tools Not Rules approach, I knew that whatever we did in the classroom, it could not be at the expense of one single student. I felt like every student could be me, dealing with a variety of personal issues and concerns. We wanted to be sure that this approach allowed *all* students to feel like they didn't need to hide, that they could own their behavior but did not need to own the shame of their circumstances.

Due to the stress in my childhood, I was drinking and smoking by twelve years old. I didn't do it because I was "bad"; I did it to cope. I was one of "those" kids—insecure and blowing up the social environment in classrooms. So, at the beginning of my career, I was determined to become the protective teacher, righteously walking with her gaggle of goslings with none left behind, even those who drove me around the bend.

When I began working with Claudia, I saw her talent for finding incredibly creative solutions to the mundane, sometimes torturous, tasks of teaching. And there is nothing more mundane and challenging than dealing with difficult behaviors. One gift of a co-teaching classroom is that one person can be working in the front of the class teaching a dazzling lesson, while one is in the back watching what is actually taking place among students. The back-of-the-classroom watcher sees amazing things, such as kicking, sleeping, craft-making, and shoe repairing. When you are one person in front of the classroom, it is impossible to see what is happening behind the scenes and desks. You do your best, but you can feel like a conductor trying to evoke music from a bag of exploding popcorn with many unpopped kernels on the bottom. Hence, this teamwork is where we freed up brain space and talent to heal what would normally be left to fester.

So, with that dynamic in place, our big breakthrough came when we were teaching Claudia's youngest child, Evy. In our elementary school, we were allowed to teach our own children. One day, after dividing the class between two rooms to work through an intensive mathematics lesson, Evy immediately fell apart with a locked-down, angry demeanor. "What? You never taught us this! I don't understand it!" he said. I told Claudia, "Evy is driving me insane."

Though I had always wanted to separate Evy's behavior from who he was, it took a mom like Claudia to make that brilliant jump as an educator. She called all the students together. "Okay, everyone in my room! We are going to brainstorm all the behaviors that bring our abilities up or down." This was the love of a mother, knowing in her heart that her son's behavior was not who he was. His behavior was just a protective mechanism, a way to cope. She didn't want me to treat him as if he was his behavior, and she made the next move.

With sixty students, we created honest lists of behaviors that brought up our skills or brought them down. From there, we constructed large posters with cut-out balloons and weights. On these cutouts, we wrote behaviors that brought our abilities up (balloons) or down (weights). Now we had something to talk about. From then on, we sent students to these posters to look for the behavior that was bringing them down, choose one that would bring it up, and then come back to us to share their insights and decisions.

Next, during a parent education evening, I was talking about essay writing, and parents were working in groups. I warned them, "Okay, no showboating in your groups!" Claudia's fierce sense of humor loved this and, in class a few days later, she stated, "We have a bunch of shirkers, workers, and showboaters in here!" And this is where it all began, with incisive creativity and the guiding light that we love *all* students, *all of them*. We started this in 2005, and since then, we have been fine-tuning and developing this essential work.

How an Idea Became Tools Not Rules

The conversations we had with students weren't about consequences; they were about *them*—how they were feeling and what behavior they might choose in a variety of circumstances. We could combine our hard-earned understanding of students with guidance and consequences, and the message was always the same: *We love you enough to not let you behave this way. So, what else can we do?* We continued to refine this work and developed three language triads to coach students.

1. Shirking, working, showboating
2. Stuck, serious, silly
3. Passive, assertive, aggressive

We created these three triads because they reflected our need to continually develop students' academic, emotional, and social maturity. We recognized that the classroom paradigm required all three sets. As much as we were teaching content and expecting academic progress, we were also solving problems from recess and helping students manage emotions that got in the way of learning. These language triads seemed to encapsulate all the circumstances involved in helping students be ready to learn. Most importantly, we clarified and visualized what *serious*, *assertive*, and *working* meant in our classroom. This language provided us with a powerful framework for helping students change their approach to learning. We became proficient at helping students be serious, assertive, and working during class. As a result, students' test scores improved. Students made leaps personally and academically that once seemed impossible. After we started using this approach regularly in the classroom, a few things happened.

1. The lofty rules we posted started becoming a reality. This did not happen through rules; it happened by allowing students to identify their own behavior and change it.

2. This approach created a classroom community where students supported each other to be a serious, assertive, working group of scholars.

3. Negative student behaviors decreased, and learning and engagement increased. As teachers, we felt more connected to students, more successful, and happier in the classroom than ever before.

At the beginning of the school year, when other teachers were going over the classroom rules, we were teaching students about honesty and how we were going to help everyone in our classroom know how to work hard, be assertive, and be serious about learning. We would even joke with students, "We have good news and bad news. The good news is that we are your teachers. The bad news is that we are your teachers!" Changing the behaviors that get in the way of learning is hard work. Over the years, we continued to refine our process, but the essentials stayed true. We recognized that to help students follow typical classroom rules, they needed the tools to do so. We have successfully used Tools Not Rules in grades 4–8 and have trained K–8 teachers to use this approach in their classrooms. From the feedback we have received, we believe that Tools Not Rules can be used to support students from kindergarten through eighth grade to self-assess and learn to manage their choices for greater academic success.

The Principles of Tools Not Rules

Tools Not Rules operates on essential principles that underpin what happens in the classroom. These principles can guide you in planning lessons, responding to sudden and chronic behavior issues, and buoying yourself from burnout. When you set TNR as a foundation, you create a novel approach to problem-solving and behavior modification, a safe space to learn and grow, and grace in your interactions with students. The six principles of Tools Not Rules include the following.

1. Honesty above anything else.
2. This approach helps everyone, not just students who struggle with disruptive behaviors.
3. Students are not their behavior.
4. If you encourage self-assessment, students are better able to self-regulate.
5. Students will be held accountable but not shamed.
6. Students are watching. They want to know how they will be treated if they have challenging behavior.

With these thoughts in mind, we want to share the following example of how we used Tools Not Rules in our classroom because it might help you and your students in similar ways. In this scenario, Ms. Gomez addresses whole-class behavior and individual behaviors that get in the way of students' working and learning. It also illuminates what Greg Wolcott, author of the book *Significant 72: Unleashing the Power of Relationships in Today's Schools* (2019) calls being "respectfully relentless." A teacher who is respectfully relentless is "constantly challenging students to go farther or reach higher while at the same time loving them up along the way" (p. 18).

Wolcott (2019) also writes that students need three things to thrive in the classroom: autonomy, belongingness, and competence. Tools Not Rules develops all three by helping students self-assess and regulate (autonomy), stay connected to other students through honest and empathetic interactions (belonging), and develop the ability to be serious, assertive workers (competency). As you read this scenario, see if you can identify these actions.

As the seventh graders filed into the classroom, their teacher, Ms. Gomez, greeted each of them at the door with a handshake, welcoming them to class. The classroom had bookshelves, potted plants, anchor charts reminding students about the key characteristics of essay writing, and a smart board at the front. This was a typical middle school classroom; however, on the back wall of the room, Ms. Gomez had hung the Tools Not Rules posters. Figure I.1 shows these posters.

Source: © 2023 by Claudia Bertolone-Smith and Marlene Moyer. Used with permission.

FIGURE I.1: Tools Not Rules posters for the classroom.

At the beginning of the year, the class engaged in learning activities that helped them understand what the language triads on the posters mean. Students knew what it meant to be shirking in class and what an aggressive reaction looked like. They brainstormed why they might choose certain behaviors, and they discussed how to shift from silly to serious if needed. Ms. Gomez used these words in class, which helped students become serious, assertive, and working on what they were learning.

Students also knew Ms. Gomez expected honesty and would not shame them for being honest about their behaviors. Students witnessed their peers making small and large mistakes (for example, talking too much, cheating on a test, stealing from the teacher's desk). They saw Ms. Gomez address all these issues using a Tools Not Rules approach. Ms. Gomez expected honesty and thanked students for being courageous enough to tell the truth. She followed through with consequences as needed. Yet, she did not allow students to tease each other for their behavior.

One time, a student stole some items off Ms. Gomez's desk. Because Ms. Gomez had been developing the norm of honesty above all else, when she asked the class to help her find out who took the items, a student let her know. Because it is middle school, the word on who did it spread like wildfire. During class the next day, the identified student's classmates started saying, "Ooooooh, you're in big trouble." Ms. Gomez immediately stopped the class and asked, "How many of you have ever stolen something?" Many students raised their hands. Then she asked, "How many of you are impressed by the courage it takes to admit you did something wrong?" All the students raised their hands. The student who stole had a consequence, but Ms. Gomez treated them with the same care and regard as all the other students. The students in this class felt safe because they knew their teacher wanted everyone to learn.

As the students sat down, Ms. Gomez commented, "I see ten out of twenty-seven students with their books out for our reading groups today. Great job; this is really assertive. Oh, and I just saw seven more students get out their books. Nice work, this shows you are serious about learning."

Ms. Gomez took attendance and began the lesson for the day. The first order of business was for students to meet in their book club groups and share their responses to reflection questions on the reading. She gave the class ten minutes to finish their questions, and when they were done with the questions, they could quietly read their choice of book.

Ms. Gomez noticed that students began chatting with each other, and a few were laughing loudly. She asked for their attention and said, "Everyone, please turn to the posters at the back of the room. Where are you right now in our work? Be honest. Choose what you are doing and tell your neighbor how you will move to serious, assertive, and working." Students looked at the posters and shared their thoughts with a neighbor.

One student said, "Well, I am being passive because I don't have my book, and I don't want to ask for one. I think I will be assertive by seeing if I can borrow one." Another student told her partner, "I am shirking. I didn't sleep a lot last night, but I think I'll start working by answering these questions."

Ms. Gomez listened to these conversations and then shared with the class, "Great. It feels like you all know what to do to start working. I'm setting a timer for ten minutes, and we will start our book club discussions when it goes off. Hard work here means you are ready with your answers to the questions. Thank you for getting started." She walked through the room, commenting, "Awesome, 80 percent of the class is working right now; that is amazing. I just saw two people end their conversations and get started; that is assertive. Keep up the good work."

Individually, she commented to a few students.

continued →

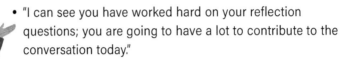

- "I noticed that you have your book and questions ready to go today; that is being a serious learner. Thank you!"

- "Yesterday, you didn't have your book, but today you do. Thank you for being assertive and making sure you had it here today."

- "I can see you have worked hard on your reflection questions; you are going to have a lot to contribute to the conversation today."

More of the class settled in, but one student, Amanda, was sitting with her head down on her desk. Amanda could be a reluctant student; she often forgot her supplies and was slow to get started. Ms. Gomez quietly approached and asked her to come see her in the hallway. Amanda got up and met her by the door. In the hall by the doorjamb, there was a set of mini posters, like the ones in the back of the room. Ms. Gomez started the conversation.

Ms. Gomez:
Hi, Amanda. Can you tell me what I value the most?

Amanda:
Yes, honesty.

Ms. Gomez:
Exactly. Where do you find honesty?

Amanda:
Right here. *(She put her hand on her chest.)*

Ms. Gomez:
True, we don't find it in our head and try to think our way to honesty; we find it in our heart to know what is honest.

Amanda:
OK.

Ms. Gomez:
I have noticed for the last few days you haven't wanted to talk with anyone, and you seem angry or upset. You haven't brought your materials with you to school either. Can you look at the posters and tell me what is going on for you?

Amanda:
Well, I am shirking and feeling a bit aggressive at the same time.

Ms. Gomez:
Thank you. Can you tell me what you need to be assertive or to get started working?

Amanda:
Well, I don't know. I just don't feel like I get what is going on. I don't like the book we are reading, and it doesn't make sense. It makes me mad.

Ms. Gomez:
Thank you so much for being honest. Is the book hard to read, or are you just unsure of what is happening in the plot?

Amanda:
No, I can read it fine. I just don't get what is happening in the book since the main character left home.

continued →

Ms. Gomez:
OK, I understand. Would it help if we found a mentor for you to talk to so they can tell you the story of what happened to the main character?

Amanda:
Well, maybe. That would help me understand.

Ms. Gomez:
Great, I know Joellee just finished reading, and she is good at explaining. Let's go work with her.

Amanda:
OK.

Ms. Gomez moved into the room with Amanda and asked Joellee if she would help. Joellee agreed, and the two students started talking. During the discussion, Ms. Gomez saw Amanda add to the conversation in her group. Ms. Gomez approached the group and said, "This group is working hard to understand the story and dig into the deeper meaning. Way to be assertive and engage in the conversation, everyone."

In a Tools Not Rules classroom, this flow of conversation is constant, relying on the language triads and an atmosphere of support, honesty, and continual focus on self-assessment and self-regulation toward becoming serious, assertive, and working. As demonstrated in the previous scenario, Ms. Gomez was prepared to address the whole class and individual students as she coached them. She was demonstrating tenacious optimism by upholding the belief that every student can be serious, assertive, and working.

With Tools Not Rules operating in the classroom, Ms. Gomez is prepared to address behaviors that get in the way of students' learning, both as a whole class and individually. When teachers use whole-class and individual praise focused on the language triads, students begin to see themselves as operating agents for change. Students also apply these ideas outside of school in playing sports, doing chores, and completing homework. This is not a fantasy classroom, and the conversations and teacher actions are real. This is what using Tools Not Rules is all about!

The Tools Not Rules Study

In order to take a closer look and gather evidence and data regarding how Tools Not Rules impacts students and teachers in the classroom, we conducted a study at a rural West Coast middle school during the 2020–2021 school year. We wanted to answer the two following questions.

1. Does Tools Not Rules help create a safe, collaborative, and supportive learning environment for students?
2. Does Tools Not Rules help students develop their self-assessment and self-regulation skills?

The study results show that Tools Not Rules can increase student and teacher autonomy, belongingness, and connection. Based on survey data collected at the beginning and end of the school year, teachers who used Tools Not Rules in their classrooms reported gains throughout the year in creating positive connections between students and staff, helping students self-regulate and choose more successful behaviors, and expecting and engaging in honest conversations with students. Compared to their peers who chose not to use Tools Not Rules in the study year, educators using TNR reported growth in collaborating with fellow staff members about effectively engaging students and supporting each other when challenged with difficult student behaviors.

We created focus groups consisting of students learning in classrooms where teachers were using Tools Not Rules. We met with them twice during the year to understand more about what they experienced when learning in a Tools Not Rules classroom. We found that the students felt a difference in classrooms with TNR; they liked being asked to self-evaluate and identify their behaviors. One focus group participant shared that they had a difficult time behaving in class, but when asked to examine their own behavior in this way, they became curious and willing to try a new approach.

Students appreciated that teachers encouraged honesty and shared that the language on the Tools Not Rules posters helped get them back on track. One student shared that when they were "spacing out," they looked at the posters for inspiration to start working again. Interestingly, students reported that using the posters to self-evaluate helped them think about their actions and how it affected their work. Overwhelmingly, students reported improving their work ethic, working harder to get their assignments done, challenging themselves in the classroom, and learning how to help themselves get back on track. To learn more about the specifics of how the study was conducted and the results, see the appendix (page 131).

About This Book

We wrote this book for grades K–8 education professionals looking for tools to help students get their behaviors out of the way of their learning and progress. Tools Not Rules is an approach to working with students and coaching them toward becoming serious, assertive, and working. As noted previously, this approach relies on the following three language triads.

1. Shirking, working, showboating
2. Stuck, serious, silly
3. Passive, assertive, aggressive

We use the language triads to support students in self-assessment and self-regulation. The triads provide students a way to self-reflect and identify what is happening for them, because sometimes students don't have the words. The words we use have been effective, but there is flexibility here for you to develop triads of your own to help your students focus on becoming serious, assertive, and working. Tools Not Rules focuses on honesty and shame-free interactions with students as essential to this work. This is why we created a poster that says: *Honesty above anything else.* The overarching goal of this approach is to help students change behaviors that are stopping them from growing academically (mastering content), socially (maintaining positive connections with others), and emotionally (self-assessment and self-regulation).

This book will guide you in learning how to use Tools Not Rules in your education space (for example, your classroom, the counselor's office, or the principal's office). We offer classroom stories (using pseudonyms to protect students' privacy) that share our underlying philosophy of how to help students make changes in behaviors that have become barriers to academic success. Following is a brief overview of each chapter.

In chapter 1, Ensuring Honesty Above Anything Else, you will learn the *why* behind how we created Tools Not Rules. We also discuss the key philosophical components of Tools Not Rules: being honest, removing shame, and recalculating the value of praise.

Chapter 2, Establishing That You Are Not Your Behavior, explores how to help students self-assess and self-regulate their choices. Separating students from their behavior allows them to easily untangle themselves from behavior choices that get in the way of learning. It reinforces the concepts of serious, assertive, and working with a new look at how to praise students.

Chapter 3, Adopting the Tools Not Rules Language, introduces the language we developed to help students assess and regulate their behavior toward success. We also share why this approach works to help student achievement and growth in the classroom.

Chapter 4, Teaching and Using the Tools Not Rules Language With Students, describes how to use Tools Not Rules language to maximize student output and engagement. Through stories and coaching, you will learn how to make this work for you and your students. We share activities to help students understand the language triads and how they can use them for self-assessment and self-regulation.

During Tools Not Rules trainings, teachers often ask about effective interventions for students who don't react well to initial efforts, who figure out new ways to exasperate us, and cause many sleepless nights. These students might need reteaching or additional support or reinforcement of both academic and behavioral skills. Chapter 5, Changing the Most Challenging Behaviors With the Start Chart, offers strategies to help build connections with the most resistant students to build trust and pathways to progress. Here we share effective ways of changing the most difficult behaviors.

In chapter 6, Overcoming Implementation Challenges and Realizing Possibilities, we reflect on possible problems and challenges you might experience in implementing the Tools Not Rules approach and offer practices and recommendations for overcoming these challenges.

Finally, in the epilogue, we share our hopes and aspirations for this work. The book concludes with an appendix, which examines the yearlong academic study conducted in a middle school with twenty teachers implementing Tools Not Rules. We share the results of the study and their implications for educational professionals and students.

Tools Not Rules does not require much material to implement. Throughout the book, we share pictures of Tools Not Rules posters that we use in our classrooms. These are available for you to order if you wish, but honestly, we made these posters by hand when we first started—using poster paper, paint, and a felt pen—and they were absolutely fine. Additionally, reproducible tools and charts are available online for your convenience (visit **go.SolutionTree.com/behavior**). We also feature a Stop & Think section in each chapter, which provides opportunities for you to reflect on and process what you are learning, providing you with some things to try with students and providing opportunities to evaluate what you learned.

Conclusion

You could choose to read this book at any time during the school year, but hopefully you do so before the school year begins, so you can be equipped with the tools and strategies you need to set the tone for a successful year. Or, maybe you have the opportunity to read this book during the summer or on winter break, with your toes in the sand or nestled into a ski boot. As teachers, our brains need time to decompress and then be ready for another school year. It is our wish that this book provides you with inspiration and new skills to build on the good work you are already doing.

We do not want this to be just another how-to book that makes you feel like there is more to do in the already daunting task of teaching. We envision you feeling more effective, engaged, and happy about each teaching day as you use Tools Not Rules. We invite you to try new things, see student behaviors in a new way, and be fully prepared to address current teaching challenges with hope and joy. From the educator in us to the educator in you—we welcome you on this journey!

Chapter 1

Ensuring Honesty Above Anything Else

> "When Maribel tripped another student, I asked her to come with me to the back of the room. 'Can you tell me what happened?' I asked. Maribel said, 'Jack wanted me to do the splits.' I said, 'I don't think that's the truth. What do I value more than anything?' Maribel pointed at the Tools Not Rules posters, saying, 'Honesty. I put my leg out to trip him.' I replied, 'Thank you for your honesty,' and gave her a hug. She hasn't been dishonest since."
>
> **J. Molesworth**, first-grade teacher, personal communication, November 19, 2023

In this chapter, we discuss the foundational principle of Tools Not Rules: *honesty above anything else*. This piece of the Tools Not Rules philosophy is essential to creating a classroom where students share the truth about what happens. Unless a classroom has this one fundamental aspect, we are unable to help students change their behaviors and trajectory in school. With the use of research, we will demonstrate why modeling honesty is equally important.

We also share an easy-to-follow method for having conversations that promote students' ability to honestly self-assess their own behavior and what is going on for them. This, in turn, supports self-regulation so behaviors can change with ease. We share actual teacher-student conversations so you can see what this looks and sounds like. Lastly, we demonstrate how the Tools Not Rules focus on honesty is directly connected to accountability that has lasting benefits.

Honesty as the Foundation

Honesty is the most important concept in Tools Not Rules, as it creates the foundation on which all other concepts and ideas are built. Without honesty, it's very difficult to make any real progress. Figure 1.1 shows an example of a poster we use in the classroom so all students can see it throughout the day. We like to put this poster above the rest to highlight that honesty is the key factor in learning to know ourselves and making necessary changes as we grow.

Source: © 2023 by Claudia Bertolone-Smith and Marlene Moyer. Used with permission.

FIGURE 1.1: Example of honesty poster.

Of all the posters we use with Tools Not Rules, this one is the most important. If you create an atmosphere of honesty where students are certain you will not shame them for telling the truth about their behaviors and their lives, then magic can happen.

Of course, we know honesty can sometimes be hard to elicit. Teachers have asked us, "What if they lie?" We can share our hard-won experience and the experience of other teachers who use this approach. If students see and hear you helping their classmates be honest and accountable for their actions without being shamed in the process, they intuit this as a safe environment built on a culture of honesty. If you regularly work with students in this way, they choose not to lie because the outcome is one of support rather than disconnection and shame. We have used Tools Not Rules for many years and can think of only two students who used lying as a defensive strategy. Throughout the year, one of those students developed the ability to tell the truth. This came slowly as the student learned to trust us as teachers and saw their peers regularly being honest.

The other student was in seventh grade by the time they arrived, and it was a COVID-19 year. By this time, the strategy of using lying to evade or gaslight a situation was a strongly developed part of their identity and how they dealt with past trauma. When we crunched the numbers, this is about .002 percent of the students we have taught.

So, what if students lie? If they do, we will work with them to develop the skills of telling the truth. Moreover, what if they tell the truth? We believe they will, under the conditions we set as their teacher. When an educator combines "honesty above all" and accountability without shame, powerful shifts in student achievement and happiness can happen.

For first graders, a teacher like Ms. Esher understands the power of honest conversations, as illustrated in this scenario.

Sophie was a spunky student who was used to things going her way. Her mom even admitted she was spoiled and cried when things weren't just as she wanted. At the beginning of the year, Sophie struggled to not tell those white lies so common in the younger grades. In Ms. Esher's class, all students receive the same black dry-erase marker. Toward the end of the year, the supply of black ones had run out and Mrs. Esher needed to give a student a purple one. Seeing this, Sophie threw out her black marker and said hers had run out too. Ms. Esher saw what was taking place and approached Sophie to try to remedy the situation.

continued →

Ms. Esher:
Sophie, may I see that marker you threw away?

Sophie:
Um no, I can't find it.

Ms. Esher:
That's OK, but what is the number-one thing we do in this classroom?

Sophie:
Be honest.

Ms. Esher:
Right, so did your marker run out, or did you want a colorful one like Mai?

Sophie:
Yeah, I just wanted a colored marker like her.

Ms. Esher:
OK, thank you for being honest. We all want different things sometimes, but I need you to use your black marker like the rest of the students.

Ms. Esher noted that Sophie had slowly matured throughout the year and changed her behavior from being overly emotional and struggling to tell the truth to being honest with ease. She also noted that honesty without shame builds trust in the classroom. Ms. Esher grew to trust Sophie's responses, and Sophie grew to trust that Ms. Esher would not disconnect from her while correcting her behavior. Ms. Esher's call-and-response chant also helped reinforce this classroom norm that being honest helps change behavior:

Ms. Esher: Class, class . . .

Students' choral response: Yes, yes . . .

Ms. Esher: Change your behavior . . .

Students' choral response: Change your life!

On some level, all of us want honest exchanges, but many of our conversations with students can inhibit truthfulness. Expecting students to be honest requires a teacher to create an environment where students are allowed to be vulnerable, admit mistakes, learn from these mistakes, and move on. If students are certain you will not shame them for telling the truth about their behaviors and their lives, then trust unfolds. Yet, sometimes, we move away from this form of vulnerability.

Brené Brown (2021) states that vulnerability is "not weakness but the greatest measure of courage" (p. 14). Brown's extensive research found that when people are vulnerable, they experience a strong sense of belonging, hope, and self-acceptance (Brown, 2011). We have found that engaging students in honest conversations without shame builds trust and connection. Classrooms and schools can foster an atmosphere of trust, connection, and belonging through careful consideration of how they communicate with students.

Honest Conversations

Tools Not Rules educators establish a foundation in their classroom for helping students see themselves separate from their behaviors. This allows them to consider what is causing the behavior and gain insight about the difficulties the behaviors are creating. Figure 1.2 (page 22) allows you to visualize the interplay of this specific conversation.

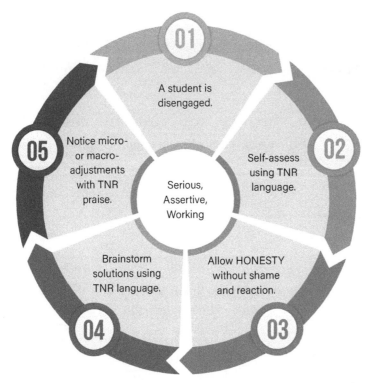

Source: © 2023 by Claudia Bertolone-Smith and Marlene Moyer. Used with permission.

FIGURE 1.2: Model of Tools Not Rules conversations and interventions for students.

The following scenario is an example of a Tools Not Rules intervention. Mr. Dao feels challenged by his student, Carlos, who constantly avoids classroom work and distracts others. He asks Carlos to step outside the classroom, and they stand together in front of small versions of the posters. This conversation happens when other students are engaged in work. This is a short conversation, taking only about ninety seconds. Notice how Mr. Dao cues Carlos to be honest, allowing him to accurately self-assess and eventually, make a different choice.

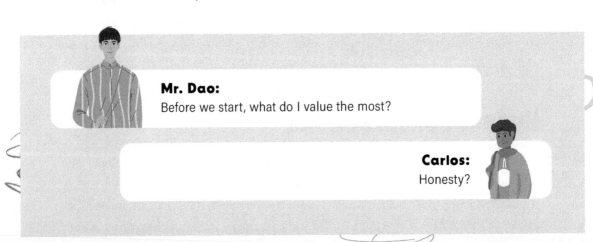

Mr. Dao: Before we start, what do I value the most?

Carlos: Honesty?

Ensuring Honesty Above Anything Else 23

Mr. Dao points to the posters to help anchor Carols, allowing space for conversation void of frustration and shaming.

Mr. Dao:
Yes, absolutely. Where do you find honesty?

Carlos:
In my heart.

Carlos puts his hand over his heart, as he has seen modeled many times.

Mr. Dao:
Right, we don't noodle our way to honesty in our head. We feel it. So, are you ready to be honest?

Carlos:
Yes.

Mr. Dao:
OK, thank you. I'd love for you to tell me what's going on. I've noticed that you have been talking during work time and not finishing your assignments. Can you look at the posters and tell me where you think you are operating from?

Carlos:
I don't know, maybe shirking and passive?

Mr. Dao:
Great, that's honest. I love that. Thank you. OK, do you have a sense of why you've been shirking and passive in class lately? What's going on for you?

continued →

Carlos:
Well, I'm not getting much sleep.

Mr. Dao:
Really, why?

Carlos:
My mom has a new baby, and he cries all the time. It takes up a lot of her time.

Mr. Dao:
That must be hard. New babies are a lot of work, and it can also make other kids feel like their parents are too busy for them.

Carlos:
Yeah.

Mr. Dao:
I hear you; the first months of a new baby are rough for everyone, and you are feeling tired too. I'm wondering what you could choose to do during class that would be assertive so you can get started working?

Carlos:
Well, I don't know how to get the right answer to the problems we are doing with angles. I get the first part, but then I always make a mistake. I also don't have my calculator today.

Mr. Dao:
OK, thank you for being honest. So, an assertive thing you could do would be . . .

Ensuring Honesty Above Anything Else 25

Carlos:
Ask someone to let me use their calculator?

Mr. Dao:
Yes, great. I can help you do that. What about knowing how to find the missing angle in the polygons?

Carlos:
Well, I wonder if I could have another copy of the notetaker where it shows all the steps on how to do the problems. I lost mine.

Carlos lost most of his notetakers, but Mr. Dao wants to celebrate here, not lecture.

Mr. Dao:
Thank you so much for your honesty and this conversation. Let's find you a calculator and get you a copy of the notetaker so you can get working. Keep me posted about the new baby in your family. I know how hard that can be.

Carlos:
OK.

Carlos follows through with working with the notetaker and using the calculator to solve practice problems. Mr. Dao stops by Carlos's desk to encourage him privately.

Mr. Dao:
I can see you are using the notetaker to help you understand; that is really assertive. Thank you.

Stop & Think

1. Take a moment to read through the dialogue again between Mr. Dao and Carlos. Did you notice the following?

    - Student self-assessment
    - Student self-regulation
    - Increased teacher and student connection
    - Honesty
    - An actionable solution supporting serious, assertive, working behavior

2. How do you think Mr. Dao felt toward Carlos at the beginning of the conversation?

3. What assumptions might Mr. Dao be making about Carlos?

4. How do you suppose Mr. Dao felt in the end?

5. How did Tools Not Rules language impact the outcome?

In *The New Art and Science of Teaching*, Robert Marzano (2017) discusses the importance of showing value and respect for reluctant learners like Carlos. Reluctant learners are challenging; they often won't engage in learning activities and refuse to do assigned work. Reluctant learners can appear anxious or rebellious. However, Marzano (2107) recommends valuing and respecting students by asking them why they feel this way during learning. When asking for an honest reason for their reluctance, a teacher can often discover important information about the student as a human being. It allows them to build a connection with trust and understanding. Valuing all students by modeling and expecting honesty before anything helps start the cycle of self-reflection and self-regulation.

For this to work, teachers must model honesty. According to Brené Brown (2012), when you say things like, "I've done that too" or "That happened to me too," you are helping eradicate shame and increase connection. This does not mean you over-disclose personal information, but rather that you are willing to present yourself as a vulnerable, imperfect human being. At the right time and, when you are comfortable sharing, you may admit that there has been a time you were not very nice to someone or cheated on an assignment. You might share that in middle school, you teased students too. You may find the moment to share an authentic experience when you were passive and should have spoken up. You might share a time when you were aggressive and dumped your anger on someone else. It is essential to leave righteousness out of the conversation.

Brown (2021) calls this *normalizing* and notes it is "one of the most powerful shame-resilience tools that we can offer our children. Normalizing means helping our children know they're not alone and that we've experienced many of the same struggles" (p. 228). Under these conditions, students have an easier time being honest about what happened and accepting the consequences. Normalizing helps students know they belong rather than believing they are the only ones who have ever done something wrong. Once students experience honesty in this way, they begin to use it more consistently in their lives.

The following story is about how Yaretzi tried honesty in our classroom and what happened when she began using it in her daily life.

One day, we had to hold one of our students, Yaretzi, accountable for being rude to a substitute teacher. The day after the substitute teacher was there, Yaretzi came in with an ice-cold handshake when greeted at the classroom door. When we asked her to talk outside, her face showed deep hurt.

We inquired, and she was forthright. "I am not mad at you for giving me detention. I am not even mad that you called my mom. I am just sad that my mom didn't even bother to tell me you called. When I was younger, she told me that when people love you, they are tough on you when you mess up. My mom didn't even mention it to me; I don't matter to her."

In this case, Yaretzi shared what was really going on, and with this, a deeper connection between us was tendered. As human beings, we know how good it can feel to come clean on something, as long as people do not disconnect from us.

Later in the school year, a student stole some food from our party supplies. We were upset and got input from other students to better understand the ease with which someone could just take what was not theirs. We asked Yaretzi, "Do a lot of kids steal?" She responded, "Yes, I steal makeup from my mom, and I stole things from a store twice. I don't do it anymore. Since I was in this class, I started being honest."

We couldn't help wondering, "Why don't you steal anymore?"

She replied, "I just feel better about myself when I am honest."

We asked, "Has it changed your relationship with your mom?"

"Oh, yes," she chirped. "She never believed me before because I lied so much. Now she knows I tell her the truth, so I can do more things. I can go out with friends, and I am

continued →

> honest with her about it all. I just feel better when I tell the truth." We were amazed at the change for this student.
>
> In trying to connect all the dots, we inquired, "So what happened with your mom not talking to you about the phone call we made?"
>
> "Well, later, she talked to me about it and asked what I did. I told her I made a bad decision. It was OK. Plus, we spend more time together now. Just me and her."
>
> Yaretzi's life changed when she started being honest.

Accountability and Honesty

Combining honesty and accountability in the classroom is a powerful tool. We can be honest about what is happening, like Yaretzi and Carlos, and make a different choice to improve our learning and our lives. But, there are behavior choices or actions that come with severe consequences. When we make poor choices, being honest about what happened and being held accountable helps us grow and change into better versions of ourselves.

Being held accountable for our behavior is a powerful lesson and can help us evolve into better human beings who are prepared for future situations and decisions. If we stop at honesty and avoid accountability, we lose the opportunity to practice how to make things right. Sometimes, we must make reparations for what we have done. This process allows us to own our transgressions and move forward in our lives with more understanding, empathy, and wisdom. As teachers, we want students to be successful but often feel stuck when their behaviors are in the way. Sometimes, we want them to "learn the hard way," or we think, "that will teach them a lesson." This often doesn't work out the way we would hope. As Brown (2012) notes, we are not open to "accepting feedback or owning responsibility for something when we're being hammered. Our hardwiring takes over and we self-protect" (p. 205). We have found that the Tools Not Rules approach to mediating negative behaviors avoids the need for self-protection and increases self-management.

When we hold students accountable and thank them for being honest, they can quickly identify their behavior and choose a more productive approach. Honesty and accountability without shame is a powerful combination. When students realize we truly want to know the truth, no matter how unpleasant it may be, they stay connected to us. This increases trust and a willingness to continue to engage in learning activities.

During a conference presentation, one participant asked if we were praising the wrong thing by thanking students for being honest about poor behavior choices. This was a great question! We have found that it is often difficult for students to be honest when they are scared, ashamed, or embarrassed about what they have done. When we thank students for being honest during a conversation, their whole demeanor changes. They are genuinely surprised and curious; they often look into our eyes, their shoulders drop, and you can see relief in their faces.

Sometimes, the hardest part is being honest about what happened, and when accountability follows, it offers a chance to make things right. Most students are all for this. We are always careful not to shame students who have been honest and followed through in making things right. We don't tease them or make sarcastic comments. This is because honest conversations with students create connections, and shame creates isolation and distrust. Instead, we show empathy for students and trust that accountability, without shame, can help them mature into making better choices. We are not praising them for their behavior; instead, we are thanking them for their *honesty* about their behavior. There is a difference, and this is when real accountability and change are possible.

Tools Not Rules for *All* Students, Striving and Advanced

As educators, we often think of behavior programs as a treatment only for students who need intervention. With Tools Not Rules, *every student* is invited to self-assess and self-regulate to reach their fullest potential. The highest academic achievers in the class sometimes feel like they need to prove they are the smartest and use "show-boating" to do it. When given a problem to solve or a passage to read, they might respond with, "I'm done" or "That's easy." This has a huge learning consequence: They often don't take the time to think through the problem or read the paragraph, and they can miss important parts of the lesson. This can be embarrassing for them when they find out they are wrong, or they missed something. It can also lead to a tenacious stubbornness, insisting they are right when, honestly, they are not.

Academically advanced students also need to practice choosing a different approach when their behavior gets in the way. This can be difficult if the student has a fixed mindset about their intelligence or abilities. This fixed mindset is the belief that intelligence is a static quantity that cannot change (Dweck, 2016). Essentially, a student who has a fixed mindset believes that if something is too difficult, there is no way to master it, as they erroneously believe they either get it or they don't. Carol Dweck (2016) also finds that students who are praised as "smart" while solving mathematics puzzles are more likely to resist trying more challenging ones and lie about the number of puzzles they solved.

On the other hand, a flexible mindset is the belief that you can develop your abilities over time through hard work and practice. In essence, a growth mindset holds the belief that we can learn and improve (Dweck, 2016). In the same study by Dweck (2016), students in another group were praised for their tenacity and ability to try different strategies to solve the same mathematics puzzles. This group challenged themselves by trying increasingly difficult tasks and were honest about their accomplishments. We share this information because even the most advanced students can develop behaviors that hold them back as well.

To illustrate this concept, we will share the story of a teacher in our school who had a student struggling in her advanced mathematics class. One day, while in another class, she vociferously announced to everyone that this teacher was the "worst teacher she'd ever had" and wanted out of her mathematics class. She told her parents and anyone else in the community who would listen. She was a gifted mathematics student and was appropriately placed in the accelerated class. Her mom set up a meeting with the teacher to allow her child to discuss what was going on. It turned out that the student felt increasingly threatened by the high-level mathematics and pace of the course. She had always been told she was smart and had never experienced a situation that required her to study, ask questions, and get things wrong.

This honest exchange opened a new opportunity and discussion about how to work hard when things get difficult, be honest if you are struggling, and be assertive and ask questions. This assured the student that feeling lost, making mistakes, and needing help is part of the learning process. Honest conversations grounded in the Tools Not Rules philosophy help students develop strategies for when they feel challenged and threatened.

Students should know what it feels like to work hard, be seriously engaged in learning activities, and be assertive in getting the things they need to succeed, regardless of their learning levels. This gives *all students* a multifaceted foundation on which to grow. At times, everyone—even adults—chooses behaviors that aren't productive for various reasons. Gifted students need to continue to develop their abilities through self-assessment and self-regulation, even when they appear to be model students. And if they are bored, it is our job to offer more challenging tasks. Our job is not to judge but to provide the right challenge and keep supporting students to adjust their behaviors toward success.

Finally, you cannot change what you do not see. When you are honest, you learn to see yourself more clearly instead of hiding the truth. You might hide yourself because you are afraid of feeling shame and disconnection. Brown wisely stated, "Guilt says we did something bad. Shame says we are bad" (Brown, 2012). Humans seek connection and community; it is a survival trait. Because of this, people tend to fear disconnection. When using Tools Not Rules, a teacher increases connection with students through honest conversations. These conversations develop connections and build relationships with students.

John Hattie (2023) investigated which intervention strategies had the greatest impact on student achievement in schools. He found that what works best is when teachers improve their interactions with students (teacher-student relationships). One of the top-ten interventions with a high effect on student achievement was developing positive teacher-student relationships (Hattie, 2023). Positive teacher-student relationships can foster two years of academic growth in one school year (Wolcott, 2019). With the Tools Not Rules approach, all students regularly self-identify their behavior in a group setting or individually. Because honesty is set up as the model, students are free to tell the truth about their thoughts and feelings. In this kind of environment, it is easier for students to be honest about what happened or what they are doing, and therefore far less threatening to try something else.

In addition to creating accountability and an honest classroom environment, Tools Not Rules is highly effective in preparing your class for greater academic achievement. In *The New Art and Science of Teaching* (2017), Robert Marzano lists highly effective teacher actions that promote student success in three overarching categories: feedback, content, and context. Context focuses on creating a classroom where students are mentally ready to learn; where students are "paying attention, energized, intrigued, and inspired" (Marzano, 2017, p. 65).

According to Marzano (2017), a highly effective learning context includes using engagement strategies, implementing rules and procedures, building relationships with students, and communicating high expectations during instruction. Tools Not Rules helps teachers establish and maintain a strong, effective, and vibrant context for learning. In fact, TNR accomplishes thirteen of the highly effective teaching actions for ensuring students are mentally ready to learn, as shown in table 1.1 (page 32).

TABLE 1.1: How Tools Not Rules Supports Marzano's Highly Effective Teaching Actions to Create a Positive Learning Context for Students

Strategies for Effective Learning Context	Highly Effective Teacher Actions Using Tools Not Rules
Using Engagement Strategies	• Noticing and reacting when students are not engaged • Increasing response rates • Providing opportunities for students to talk about themselves • Motivating and inspiring students
Implementing Rules and Procedures	• Establishing rules and procedures • Organizing the physical layout of the classroom • Demonstrating *withitness* • Acknowledging adherence to rules and procedures • Acknowledging a lack of adherence to rules and procedures
Building Relationships	• Using verbal and nonverbal behaviors that indicate affection for students • Understand students' backgrounds and interests • Displaying objectivity and control
Communicating High Expectations	• Demonstrating value and respect for reluctant learners

Source: Adapted from Marzano, 2017.

Hattie (2023) states that making connections with students is a very powerful teaching tool. This means that in addition to teaching content, teachers must connect with students. Wolcott (2019) also finds that when teachers experience strong, positive relationships with their students, they feel more effective, happy, and satisfied with their work. Tools Not Rules can support teachers in creating and maintaining a highly effective context in which students thrive. It's a win-win!

Stop & Think

Think of a moment when you were dishonest about your behavior. How might things have changed if you had been honest? What was the cost to you for your dishonesty?

Conclusion

This chapter shared the fundamental underlying principle of Tools Not Rules: *honesty above anything*. If students feel they can be honest, they are more encouraged to foster connections and positive relationships. This approach builds flexible mindsets in students around behavior and the freedom to be honest. Brown (2016) states that guilt can help us recognize that a behavior is wrong, and we can make amends. Shame, on the other hand, makes students believe they *are* their behavior, and then honesty and accountability become difficult. When a student feels shamed, they believe you are rejecting *them*, not just their behavior. This can degrade the student-teacher relationship.

However, when an educator combines *honesty above all* and accountability without shame, powerful shifts in student achievement and happiness can happen. In the next chapter, we discuss how to use the Tools Not Rules approach to make sure students understand they are not their behavior. This involves removing shame and staying connected to students even during episodes of behavior intervention. This sets the stage for an honest, shame-free, self-assessing, and self-regulating classroom.

Try This!

Take note of how you approach students to discuss behaviors that get in the way of their work. Try a "mini" Tools Not Rules approach with a student. Share that you value honesty above anything. Describe what you see and ask them what is going on. Make a space for them to be honest without a negative reaction. Thank them for their honesty and ask how you can help get them working. Help them get started.

If you see even a microshift toward working, let the student know you noticed by pairing the behavior with the Tools Not Rules word: "I see you are (label the action, such as *asking questions*) so you can do your lab correctly. This is (label the TNR behavior, such as *assertive*) and important as a scientist." After your conversation with the student, ask yourself the following questions.

1. How did your conversation with the student go?
2. What did you learn about them that you might not have known before?
3. What was it like when you asked them to be honest? Do you think it worked?
4. How did this exchange feel to you? Did your feelings change from beginning to end?

Chapter 2

Establishing That You Are Not Your Behavior

> "Kids come with their labels or baggage and then see that label as their identity. Tools Not Rules allows them to get away from that label and reflect on their actions. They believe certain things about themselves, and now that can change."
>
> **J. Gonzalez**, teacher, grade 6 two-way bilingual social studies and grades 7–8 ELD, personal communication, November 17, 2023

It is important to separate students from their behavior. When you do this, you allow them some breathing room from the labels that may have plagued them before they got to your classroom. It also allows you, the teacher, a space to understand more about where students' behavior originates. Having an honest conversation about what is going on with students provides insight into what drives their behavior. It also helps you support them in choosing a different behavior.

This chapter examines the price of shame and the power of connection. Additionally, it discusses a winning classroom and sports philosophy exemplified by Tools Not Rules. When a teacher has a predictable, connection-based process to follow, it puts other students at ease and builds trust within the classroom. We also provide real classroom scenarios in which teachers move away from shame-based interactions by transforming them into opportunities to create connections.

A Different Approach to Behavior

We can unequivocally state this: *We are not our behavior*. We can also say this with the same assurance: *Our behavior can create a hot mess of our lives*. The place between these two spots is where we are creating a space with Tools Not Rules—between behavior and outcomes. As educators, if we do not treat students like they are good or bad or could lose their standing at any moment, then there is hope and space to breathe. There is space to self-assess, self-regulate, and be honest. And then, outcomes change.

Many teachers struggle with managing behavior, and what they used in the past may not be working with this generation of students. We propose that behavior is a symptom of something that must be excavated by the student with the help of educators. To do this, teachers need to understand what is beneath the behaviors and be guided to choose a different approach. This mirrors how educators teach, reflect, and refine. Classrooms that are anchored in honesty, without shame, can change students' lives. These environments can make us happier and less stressed teachers in the process. We know from nearly fifteen years of working with this approach that if students know we will stay connected with them through their worst behaviors, they choose to be honest and more responsible.

As educators, however, we are aware that sometimes what drives a student's behaviors can be very difficult situations. It is not uncommon for a teacher to hear that there is possible abuse, neglect, financial challenges, or divorcing parents at home. At this point, it is best to bring in other professionals who can check in with the student. You might say, "I'd like to share this with the counselor or social worker so they can check in with you." This way, your school can start supporting this student in more significant ways that require more expertise, time, and attention. Even if a student says they do not want to share things with other adults, it is important to engage the team and let them know that this student needs support. Teachers often do not have the time in the classroom to delve into what is taking place in a student's home life. As always, if it seems like it could be serious, it is essential to reach out to others who can offer more specialized attention.

As noted previously, students can become overly identified with their behaviors, sometimes believing that the behaviors are part of who they are as a person. This requires us to help them see the space between their actions (behaviors) and how they label themselves. These reactions, as well as the reactions of others in the classroom, can impact their mindset regarding what they can achieve academically. As educators, we can help students develop a growth mindset through self-assessment and trying different behaviors that produce increasingly positive results.

Actions, Not Labels

When a student comes to your classroom with behavior baggage, they often feel that they *are* their behavior and engage in self-talk, such as the following.

- "I am the 'bad' kid."
- "I am the one who never does their work."
- "I am the one who always finishes first."
- "I am the one who doesn't ever pay attention."
- "I am bored in all my classes."
- "I am . . ."

When students hear teachers, family members, and peers talk about their behavior and academic progress in the classroom, this can form what Wood (2013) calls a *macro-identity*. A macro-identity becomes stable and can impact the student's narrative of what they can and cannot accomplish. It also can cause a thickening of their identity (Wortham, 2008), making it increasingly difficult to shift their self-perception.

When we started this work, we used the Tools Not Rules language as nouns—*shirker, showboater, worker,* and so on. However, we quickly realized we needed to change these words to verbs—*shirking, showboating, working.* This allowed us to focus on *actions*, not labels. Instead of seeing students as sweet or resistant or challenging, we recognized that they often chose behaviors based on what they thought was happening ("Everyone gets this science experiment except me.") and emotions ("I hate science! It makes me feel stupid!"). The ensuing behavior could be putting their head on the desk (stuck), goofing around with all the science equipment (silly), or shouting at their group members (aggressive). Their behavior is a way of communicating what is going on with their own thinking and feelings, albeit ineffectively. Helping students choose a different behavior in response allows for quick adjustments that can make a huge difference.

Educators can also learn from Victor Frankl (1959), a Holocaust survivor who lived in a concentration camp during World War II. Even in these extreme circumstances, Frankl found a space within him where he could *choose* his behavior and his outlook. In turn, even under the great duress of his situation, he found the autonomy to take responsibility in choosing actions. He describes this space of choice as the tension between freedom and responsibility (Frankl, 1959).

Similarly, Anthony Bandura's social learning theory (1977) includes the idea of a space where we consider the tension between freedom and responsibility and reward and punishment. His theory suggests there is a cycle that occurs when children choose behaviors. The cycle includes an *environmental input* (the teacher asks students to take out their computer and start working on their essays), a *mediational process* (Do I want to do this? What will happen if I do? What will happen if I don't? What happened the last time I didn't? I hate working on the computer; I can never find where we are working.), and *behavioral output* (I pretend I can't find my computer and when I do, I'm just going to mess around because I'm frustrated.).

This mediational process, or space, which occurs between environmental input and behavioral output is where Tools Not Rules intervenes. We separate students from their behavior when we do the following.

- **Reflect on what we see during their output:** For example, "I noticed that when it is time to take out our computers and work, you seem resistant and need a lot of reminders."
- **Ask about environmental input:** For example, "What is going on for you? Do you know why this happens?"
- **Revisit the space (mediational process):** For example, "What can you do to get the information about where our work is? Who might be able to help you at your table? Can I help you find a mentor?"

When you separate students from their behavior in this way, something magical occurs. It creates cracks in their thickened identities and helps them shed unhelpful and damaging behavior. They have the freedom to assess where they are and take responsibility for their actions. We have found time and time again that students take responsibility and change. As Frankl (1959) states, "Every human being has the freedom to change at any instant" (p. 131). Tools Not Rules allows students and teachers to create and experience that space to choose differently and affect outcomes. When you assure students that they are not their behavior, you affirm that the behavior needs to be addressed, but *who they are* is still emerging and learning—and accepted.

Growth Mindset

Maintaining an open and flexible mind refers to Dweck (2016) and her discussion of the growth mindset. Having a growth mindset about students' capability to change their behavior creates a significant change in a teacher's approach, moving away from shame, reward, and punishment to fostering a strong relationship and support system for every student (Romero, Robertson, & Warner, 2018). When we get to this place, we get to do the good work of helping students figure out who they are and what their own unique and important potential might be.

Over the ten years we taught together, we witnessed this shift repeatedly. For example, a student would acknowledge that they wouldn't start on their literacy tasks because they were afraid people would find out they couldn't read very well. And, even more frightening, their friends might think they were dumb. This was honest, and we thanked them for sharing their thoughts with us. Note that we didn't try to talk them out of their personal assessment with comments like, "Oh, no, you are so smart. You aren't dumb." This is because the fear of not being good enough is real. Often, the solution is to help them get started, get working and thinking, so they know they are capable.

Students in this situation would often either agree to get started and ask a question if they got stuck or choose a partner who they felt was working hard with the reading and analysis. We guided them in choosing partners because, at first, we found they would pick their best friends, which resulted in lots of shirking and not much working. This is what we call a *stalemate*—someone with whom your thinking and working go "stale" because you are so invested in the social dynamic. Instead, we helped students choose hardworking partners and had an honest conversation with them, establishing what kind of help was needed.

This one shift in behavior—from a student who won't do their reading work to a student who is getting started and has support when they get stuck—makes a huge difference. Even a small change can cascade into a significant shift. It is akin to putting your oar in the water when steering a raft—one small, intentional stroke can send you in a different direction, and the journey can completely change.

This teacher-student conversation gives students space to evaluate the situation. It suspends the need to keep forging on with the behavior and allows students to understand what is happening and try something different. There may be a consequence for behaviors; however, the connection between student and teacher is preserved, which is key to helping students make lasting changes while continuing to learn.

As a teacher friend stated, "If you can change your behavior, you can change your life." We continue to witness this positive cycle (see figure 1.2, page 22) repeatedly.

A historical approach to managing students was often physical (or corporal) punishment, as in "Spare the rod, spoil the child!" This was widely accepted in schools. Once corporal punishment was eradicated from the classroom, teachers often resorted to shaming. When students are rude, defiant, refuse to work, or demonstrate behaviors that stop the class from learning, teachers need to do something. Unfortunately, teachers might use shame because they are tired of the behavior, and they just aren't sure what else to do. Yet, shame has a high cost.

Brené Brown's groundbreaking work on shame illustrates how dangerous it can be to children of all ages. According to Brown (2021), shame is an "intensely painful feeling or experience of believing that we are flawed and therefore unworthy of love and belonging" (p. 137). It is important to recognize that shame in the school setting can disconnect students from content, teachers, and often school altogether (Sommers, Unigarro, Vantassel, Bertolone-Smith, & Puliatte, 2022). Students in this situation can check out either physically (drop out) or mentally (refuse to try).

Brown (2021) claims that shame needs three things to thrive: (1) secrecy, (2) silence, and (3) judgment. If we, as educators, rely on shame to modify student behavior, we may get a student who disconnects, goes silent, and feels unworthy. We may get a student who feels angry, resistant, or who works hard to disrupt learning. Shame disconnects students from teachers, and if students don't trust you, it also disconnects them from the content you teach.

Claudia Bertolone-Smith, Allison Puliate, Samantha Dale, Michele Unigarro, and Danielle Vantassel (2023) investigated preservice teachers' relationships with mathematics by asking them to write a letter directly to mathematics. They found that participants often mentioned negative emotions toward mathematics in conjunction with classroom environments that emphasized competition (or timed-test prizes) and teachers who used sarcasm or demonstrated insensitivity to students needing more help in the subject.

Moreover, Wolcott (2019) calls teaching strategies that erode student trust and positive relationships "connection killers" (p. 26). These include sarcasm, lack of empathy, having teacher's pets, public shaming, and class hierarchy (for example, posted grades or behavior charts so everyone knows where they stand). Interestingly, the preservice teachers in the study reported that they often refused to participate in class activities or do their work in classrooms using connection killers.

Take a minute with this—Brown (2021) claims that when people are shamed for what they do, they feel unworthy of love and belonging.

> **Stop & Think**
>
> Think of your own school experience. Did a teacher shame you? What happened to your sense of belonging and connectedness to the teacher? What happened to your ability to learn content from this teacher? Do you still carry those feelings today?

Positive Student-Teacher Relationships

We created Tools Not Rules for teachers so they could move toward offering students more connection and less shame. This is part of building strong and supportive relationships. Eric Jensen (2019) notes the high value of student-teacher relationships as a catalyst of strong academic achievement. If you want students to continue to learn, you must attend to your relationships and connections with them. We are not saying we are bad educators when we resort to shame, nor that we don't want the best for our students. However, the reliance on shame to motivate is undermining the very thing we want for students—*their success*!

Bessel Van Der Kolk (2014) writes that people carry stories in their bodies. He says that we feel these stories are true and that they are part of who we are. You, too, have your own stories of shame or support from teachers. These stories stay with us. They tell us who we are and who we are capable of being. With that understanding, educators have a unique opportunity to build a story for all students that they are worthy of connection and capable of amazing things. Isn't that what we all want? We want someone to believe in us, even when our behavior is disrespectful or rude; we want someone who is not afraid to hold us accountable because they believe in our worth. Educators can keep social and academic expectations high while showing great regard for students.

According to Zaretta Hammond (2015), this type of educator is called a "warm demander." In this role, teachers need to create the right balance between becoming an "ally in the learning partnership" where educators need to know "when to offer emotional support and care and when to not allow the student to slip into learned helplessness" (p. 97). Hammond (2015) follows this passage by cautioning that it is easy to think that just being firm and authoritarian is the key to increasing achievement for marginalized students. She emphasizes that personal warmth and active demandingness must go hand in hand. With Tools Not Rules we argue that this is essential. This combination of warmth and high-achievement goals is what students desperately need to combat their isolation, low self-confidence, high distraction, and disconnection.

Let's look at a winning approach in the world of sports. Nick Saban, former football head coach at the University of Alabama, has won seven national championships and numerous national coach of the year awards. In a 2023 YouTube interview, Saban reveals that he tries to change his players' behaviors without being punitive. This is a focus on creating connection versus shame. Saban (2023) states that "most of us did something in life that wasn't a great choice, [but] we want to educate players about what they did and learn [from it]."

Saban is highly focused on accountability that always creates a path to offer second chances. He believes expectations are a premeditated way to create disappointment; instead, he stays process oriented. Most importantly, he focuses on players' lives after football—he wants them to build skills during their college years that help them have healthy and productive post-college lives. Saban shares that his success in helping players prepare for their lives after football is the thing he is proudest of, not of winning games. Saban finds that this approach has better results than heavy punishments riddled with negativity. Coach Saban's process-focused formula develops lasting, productive connections, relationships, and, ultimately, greater success (Saban, 2023).

Saban's work deeply resonates with the Tools Not Rules philosophy. His winning style includes a focus on humility. He emphasizes that we all make mistakes, acknowledges the importance of accountability without shame, and gives opportunities to try again. This coincides with the belief that who we are is not our behavior. Of course, behavior can cause problems, but he focuses on pathways to better outcomes.

With Tools Not Rules, we deeply believe in this process of self-assessment and self-regulation because, like Coach Saban, we are looking toward students' futures in the world after school, not just test scores. Students must continue to build the skills to identify and change their behavior when needed. Most importantly, as with Saban, we want them to have a healthy and satisfying future, and behavior is a huge part of that.

Now, let's move off the playing field and into the classroom. In every interaction you have with students, you can choose connection over disconnection. Consider the following real-life examples in which you might disconnect. Then, reenvision those same interactions with a focus on connection and accountability without shame.

The following scenarios describe various challenges you might encounter in the classroom. Each scenario is followed by a list of ways you might react and the possible outcomes, including disconnection oriented, connection oriented, accountability, and Tools Not Rules rationale.

- **Scenario 1: A Student Often Comes to Class Late**
    - *Disconnection oriented:* You ignore them because you are so annoyed that they are late *once again*. You might grunt a reasonable greeting with no warmth, such as, "Open your book," "Get to work," or "Ask a neighbor."
    - *Connection oriented:* You give a warm greeting *every single morning*, such as, "I am so glad you are here." Have a private conversation with the student, asking what is happening at home. Genuinely wonder about their behavior with them. What could it be about? What do you notice? What is it connected to?
    - *Accountability:* In this case, accountability may come from the policy your school has in place. If, through your honest conversations with a student, you learn that their tardiness is due to hardships with home and family that are beyond their control, we recommend using extended support services your school may offer to help address this situation. When a student experiences this kind of support, it may motivate them to become more assertive at home about the importance of attending school.

        While accountability is important, if the consequence is punishing a student for something out of their control, they might feel ashamed. They may also disconnect from educators and education, which is not the intended outcome of having high expectations.
    - *TNR rationale:* Students will work harder for anyone who shows them positive attention. "Children (and adults) will do anything for people they trust and whose opinion they value" (Van Der Kolk, 2014, p. 352).
- **Scenario 2: An Angry Student Is Rude and Interrupts Instruction All Day**
    - *Disconnection oriented:* Keep saying the student's name repeatedly in multiple ways to redirect them. You are trying to say it with warmth, but you are seething and

tired underneath the veneer. "Jamie, please get your pencil off the floor."

This is another correction about negative behavior. You do this because they need redirection, but every interaction is negative, and the student knows it.

- *Connection oriented:* Take the student outside with empathy and without emotional overlay. Ask with genuine curiosity what might be going on. Ask how you can help. For a moment, try to remember what it is like to act out. Thank the student for their honesty. (See chapter 6, page 107, for approaches to support that 5 percent of extreme cases that seem impossible to help.)

  Sometimes, a student's struggle may be about you, and you must be able to hear that. If you receive hard feedback, do not defend it. Thank the student for their honesty. Take a moment to yourself to see if you can change some part of the interaction that is causing a reaction. Remember, students bring a long history into your classroom. It is often not fully about you but their history. And, if it is something you can change, find a way to reestablish the connection.

- *Accountability:* Call the student's parents or guardians. You can assign detention. However, no matter what you do, focus on remaining connected by having honest conversations about what you notice, and allow the student to share with you what is happening with them.

- *TNR rationale:* If you have created an honest classroom, students will tell you the truth. You will not make all the headway you want, but you will maintain connections with students who have most likely already given up on themselves. These students will work harder for you.

- **Scenario 3: A Student Never Does Their Work**
    - *Disconnection oriented:* You stop engaging, knowing that the work will not get done. As teachers, we often admit that we have "given up." You tell them to check their grades and finish the assigned work.

      This doesn't feel shame oriented, but it makes students feel like they are unworthy of your effort or human connection; they are worthless.

If you leave this situation as status quo, the student doesn't work, and you will become increasingly frustrated. You throw the book at them—in-school suspension, meetings with parents, out-of-school suspension, a failing grade in the class—and still, the student doesn't work.

- *Connection oriented:* Take the student to the side. Remind them that you love honesty. Ask them what is happening to them at home or school. Ask them how you can help. Most likely, they will start doing some of the work.

- *Accountability:* The student's grade may remain low. You are not there to fake that effort has taken place. However, you can be creative. Find other ways to assess their performance. Show flexibility and a willingness to meet them where they are.

- *TNR rationale:* Even if the student doesn't do the work, they know that they are still worthy of your regard. This is no small achievement. Imagine what the student feels in all their other classes or at home. Plus, you will find that you like this student more because you feel like you have an honest exchange, you understand more about them, and you are not taking the behavior personally. All of this helps improve your overall happiness in your job. When you ask students what is going on in their lives and invite them to reflect on it, you open a world of possibilities.

Students often describe themselves as "the dumb one" or "the one who never does anything," and they enjoy the status quo. You can offer the opportunity for them to try something new and see what happens. Though this might seem like a small gesture, it can begin to dramatically shift the nature of your relationship once the connection has begun. Students will feel hopeful, and they will work for you.

When students can identify their behavior and self-regulate, there is accountability. This typically prevents a teacher from wanting to punish students who have offended them. They often move to anger, shame, or apathy when they feel students aren't pulling their weight. In other words, "Why should I care more than they do?" One reason we, as educators, should care more than students do is because we are adults, and they are children.

We need to stick with them as they work out behavior that can deeply impact how they see themselves as learners.

- **Scenario 4: A Student Is Cheating or Plagiarizing**
    - *Disconnection oriented:* Point out cheating and plagiarizing. Write up the students and give them a zero. Show your disappointment by disconnecting from them. On some level, we take this personally or just think of the student as a loser or bad.
    - *Connection oriented:* Ask the student what you love above anything. Tell them they find honesty in their feelings, not their head. Ask them if they cheated or plagiarized. If you have set up a classroom where students believe you want to hear the truth, most students will be honest. Thank them for their honesty. Point out that you know when students cheat or plagiarize, it is not because they are bad, it is because they are nervous or afraid. Ask them why they were nervous about this assignment. If they come up blank, take some earnest guesses yourself, such as, "Did you feel like you couldn't do it? How long have you felt like this? In what grade did it start?"
    - *Accountability:* Do not give a score for the assignment but instead, offer to let the student do the assignment again. If they do not have the skills to do all of it, meet them where they are so you can get a clear picture of what they *do* know. Standards-based grading offers a clear path forward for this approach (Heflebower, Hoegh, Warrick, & Flygare, 2018). If no work is completed, refer to your school's grading policy.
    - *TNR rationale:* You are trying to connect with students to help them get to the place where they will show you some work. Of course, they may never do the assignment again, but you have not made their suffering worse. Your conversation will get a deeper understanding and create empathy. It will help the student be honest about something they most likely have never been honest about in their lives. As Jensen (2019) shares, you create emotional safety by ensuring students' voices are respected.

Students Are Watching

There was a student at the middle school where we both taught in single-subject classrooms—we will call him Bryan. Bryan's behavior wrecked any attempt at instruction and learning. The school had adopted a positive behavior intervention-type system (for example, carnival tickets for good behavior), and the administration insisted this would fix unexpected school behaviors. Positive behavioral interventions and support (PBIS) systems have been a hopeful system for addressing troublesome behaviors; however, a study of five districts showed that PBIS became a mechanism for restoring order and compliance in disruptive students rather than building justice or community (Bornstein, 2017).

Unfortunately, Bryan made a mockery of the system and proved to us how ineffective it can be. Bryan was a student in Tier 3 behavior intervention who experienced multiple adverse childhood experiences before first grade. No behavior plan, reward, consequence, or support seemed to make a difference. Teachers complained about Bryan because of their frustration and lack of tools and support for dealing with his behaviors. They worried about the quality of instruction for other students, too. We imagined that the other students in the class were just as frustrated with Bryan for being so disruptive. Claudia's niece, Ellie, was in several classes with Bryan, and she was serious about school. We thought Ellie must be completely aggravated by the magnitude of learning disruption Bryan caused. We knew from her teachers that they were frustrated with his behavior too.

When we asked Ellie about the situation, she shared that she liked Bryan. She said he was funny and often kind. From her perspective, teachers misunderstood Bryan's behavior, and she didn't think they were helping at all. Ellie did not watch Bryan's behavior as much as she watched teachers' reactions to it. *This is an important point.* Bryan was not letting her down; instead, Ellie felt the teachers were falling short on how to help and missing the opportunity to connect with the tender and good parts of Bryan.

Sometimes, as teachers, we think that the rest of the students will be pleased if we punish and shame the offending student. Through our Tools Not Rules work, we have realized that it has the opposite effect. Research supports that creating and maintaining a school climate based on collaboration, high-quality social and emotional interactions in the classroom, and supporting students and teachers can lead to greater academic progress and social maturity (Hattie, 2023; Marzano, 2020; Reyes, Brackett, Rivers, White & Salovey, 2012).

We heard similar stories from students in our Tools Not Rules study (see the appendix, page 131), which surprised us as well. Students in classrooms that used TNR shared that they liked knowing what was going to happen to a student if they were having a bad day, and their behavior showed it. They reported that there was safety in the process. They knew the teacher would talk to the students and ask what was going on. The words the teacher would use were posted on the wall: *passive-assertive-aggressive*, *shirking-working-showboating*, and *silly-serious-stuck*. The teacher would refer the student for further consequence if needed, and when the student returned, the teacher would welcome them back again without any grudge, residual anger, or frustration.

We discovered that students were watching us, and they wanted to know, "What would happen if I got caught cheating on an assignment, shouted at a teacher, or forgot my homework?" Students are satisfied when they see teachers treat their friends with respect and empathy and follow through on consequences they have seen consistently implemented over and over. Research shows that establishing procedures for dealing with behavior in the classroom helps everyone feel more physically safe and emotionally supported (Marzano, Warrick, Rains, & DuFour, 2018). Tools Not Rules gives teachers a way to consistently address behaviors and show—not just tell—students they are safe, will remain connected, will be held accountable, and will not be shamed.

We close this chapter with a story that illustrates the power of shame-free accountability, self-assessment, and self-regulation.

Sarah came into our class like a tornado. She was in constant motion: fidgeting with things, walking around the room, or performing gymnastics moves in the corner by the cubbies. She was often engaged in "recess warfare" and was slippery when it came to doing schoolwork. We couldn't get her to complete anything. She was great at looking like she was working, reading, calculating, and staying on task; however, when we checked on her, we could tell there was something not quite right.

Sarah had been to several different schools before ours, and it was unclear what her achievement levels were. It appeared that Sarah could get class mathematics work done but couldn't pass tests. She preferred working with partners, and then it dawned on us that her strategy for success was to have her partners do her work. We taught fifth grade, and when we tested Sarah in mathematics, she was at a first- to second-grade level.

It became clear that what we were doing was too difficult for her, and she had developed a sophisticated strategy to get by. We talked with Sarah about this and asked for honesty above everything else. We wanted to know what was going on with her mathematics work. She burst into tears and admitted that she was getting students to do the work for her. She was scared because it was too hard, and she didn't want her friends to know. She had a lot of social capital. When we told her that we could set up a situation where she participates in our mathematics lessons but works on mathematics at her level—she was interested. We also asked her how she would like to break her habit of asking students to do her work, as it was a well-oiled routine.

Since we had class meetings every morning, it wasn't unusual for both classes to gather to discuss things together. Sarah decided she wanted to talk to her classmates at a class meeting. There are moments in your teaching career that you will never forget, and we will always remember this one.

At the class meeting, we crowded together in a circle of fifty students and two teachers. We all sat on the floor, and Sarah began talking. She said, "I want to tell you all that I ask you to do my work in mathematics because it's really hard for me. I don't get it, and I just want to turn in the finished work. But I also want to tell you that I do want to learn mathematics. Ms. Moyer and Ms. B are going to let me work on different mathematics during work time. So, I want to ask you not to do my work, even if I ask. Don't cheat for me because I want to learn."

The class sat silently, and we asked them, "Who has ever cheated? Raise your hand." About thirty hands flew into the air. "Who admires Sarah for the courage it took to share this with us?" All hands were raised. Some students pledged their support; some shared that they cheated too. We ended the meeting, and the students walked out to recess. We were stunned. What just happened?

Sarah spent the rest of the year working through an ability-matched mathematics curriculum and practicing grade-level curriculum with the class. School never was easy for her, but she was learning to be serious, assertive, and working, and that was important. Years later, we saw Sarah's mom in town. We asked her how Sarah was doing, and she said, "You two were the only teachers who ever really saw Sarah. She made the most progress in your class. She still talks about it all the time."

Using regular classroom meetings, or circles, is a wonderful way to foster "relatedness, accountability, and healthy interpersonal skills" (Romero et al., 2018, p. 87). As demonstrated in Sarah's story, the classroom meeting offered a safe place for a restorative approach to addressing an important issue.

According to Abraham Maslow (1943), having friends, feeling accepted, and having a sense of connection is essential to the need for love and belonging. Students experience the synergy of self-actualization when they develop a desire to become the best that they can be (McLeod, 2023). We can support students on the journey to self-actualization by being aware of the side effects of shame and being tenaciously optimistic that each student in your class can live up to their potential, and you can help them get there.

Conclusion

With Tools Not Rules, we work hard to separate students from their behavior. We do this by having students assess their behavior with the behavior triad posters. We create honest exchanges that help us, and the students understand their behavior more clearly. From this, we create stronger relationships that allow students the opportunity to adjust their unproductive actions, and from that, we feel more successful in our role as educators. From this predictable process, students feel safe, and they trust the process will unfold as they have seen it done time and time again.

In the next chapter, we discuss adopting the language of Tools Not Rules, and the power of using this approach in your classroom and, if possible, your whole school. Once we created the three triads, it was so much easier to flow into conversations with students and quickly have an effective conversation. Students became very familiar with the Tools Not Rules vocabulary, which limited confusion. We use the triads to help students identify their behavior and choose a new approach.

Try This!

Start noticing your interactions with students and other children when you need to redirect or address difficult behaviors. What is your approach to correcting students? Where do you feel successful? What would you like to change? See if you can shift a shame-oriented situation to a connection-oriented one. What happened? Would you try this again?

Chapter 3
Adopting the Tools Not Rules Language

> *What I love is when students start using the Tools Not Rules language. I overhear them talking to friends or when doing a weekly reflection on work habits. It has added to their vocabulary on discussing their own personal behaviors.*
>
> **R. Reading**, teacher, grade 7 ELA and grades 6–8 ELD, personal communication, November 19, 2023

What we say in the classroom matters. We might think that some students never hear us or aren't paying attention, but they are! There are several benefits of having an established language to discuss behavior and approaches to working with students. First, it is a well-defined framework you can lean on during surprising or difficult situations. Teachers and administrators have shared that the TNR posters and language are crucial when dealing with surprising or frustrating student behaviors. They take a moment to breathe, look up at the posters, and begin the conversation with the student, "I appreciate honesty above anything else. Can you help me understand what is happening?"

or "I've noticed that when it is time to start our mathematics work on the computer, you struggle to get started. Can you look at the posters and tell me what is going on for you?" This allows a break in student-teacher tension and may offer a way forward.

Second, when you use the language consistently, students start to expect it, reflect more deeply on their behavior using the triads, and know that the teacher will stay in this framework for the interaction. This creates a foundation for emotional safety and often inspires hope and growth for both teachers and students.

In this chapter, you will learn the meaning of the words we use in Tools Not Rules and how to use them effectively in your classroom. By exploring real-life experiences and scenarios, you will understand how the power of common language works among administrators, teachers, and students. You also will discover how a predictable pathway, with established language, allows teachers and students to get back on track quickly. Lastly, you will learn why the Tools Not Rules language and process helps schoolwide and districtwide behavior initiatives become more effective.

The Meaning of Tools Not Rules Language

It is important to know what we mean when we use Tools Not Rules language. When introducing the three-word triads to students or teachers, be aware that some may not be sure of their intended meanings. Figure 3.1 provides the words, their meanings, and examples to help clarify any confusion or misconceptions.

In class, we color-coded the words on the posters to match data revealed in brain research about students' stress levels.

- Where are you operating from?
    - Shirking (blue)
    - Working (green)
    - Showboating (orange)
- When things get difficult, I get . . .
    - Stuck (blue)
    - Serious (green)
    - Silly (orange)
- Choose your approach.
    - Passive (blue)
    - Assertive (green)
    - Aggressive (orange)

Adopting the Tools Not Rules Language

Where Are You Operating From?

Word	Meaning	Example
Shirking	The student knows what they are supposed to do but chooses not to. Shirking sometimes serves to hide the fact that they are confused and not sure what to do or are angry for another reason.	Maria does not start the science assignment. She heard the teacher say to complete the worksheet, but she keeps drawing on her binder. "I am not going to do it," she thinks.
Working	The student understands the task and is completing it.	In group work, Jo is taking charge and asking for input from others to ensure everyone knows what they need to do. After some discussion, she clarifies a point with the teacher.
Showboating	The student is trying to get outside attention at an inappropriate time.	Jack keeps waving his hand to answer every question. He states loudly how easy it is for him.

When Things Get Difficult, I Get . . .

Word	Meaning	Example
Stuck	The student knows the work is difficult and sits in their seat doing nothing. The student wants to get started but doesn't know what to do for the next step.	Carlos doesn't know where to start and just sits there when everyone around him is working. He feels miserable.
Serious	The student knows the work is challenging yet stays engaged by asking questions, reading the instructions, and getting to work.	Jacqueline isn't sure what to do, so she finds a mentor to help her. Once she completes one question, she checks back in to see if her work is correct.
Silly	When the work gets challenging, the student is making fun or trying to get laughs from others.	Corbin has always struggled in mathematics. Once work starts, he continually tells jokes to his shoulder partner.

FIGURE 3.1: Tools Not Rules word triads.

continued →

Choose Your Approach

Word	Meaning	Example
Passive	The student sits quietly to avoid letting others know that they do not know how to complete the task.	Izzy doesn't know what to do but won't raise her hand. She doesn't have the self-confidence to say she doesn't know. She has repeated this pattern over and over again. Silence is better than being embarrassed.
Assertive	When the student is unclear or confused about an activity or concept, they politely raise their hand for the teacher or ask others for help until they are clear on what to do and how to do it.	Eduardo doesn't have the paper everyone else has. As soon as he notices, he raises his hand to politely ask for one. Since he lost a little time, he asks a mentor to help him get started.
Aggressive	The student uses direct or indirect anger to address academic or social issues that challenge them.	Khristal rarely participates in the learning. When the teacher asks her to sit down, another student snickers. Khristal reacts by shouting across the room, "What are you laughing at?" posturing for a fight. She sits down and slams her fist on the desk, crosses her arms as if to say, "I won't do anything in this class."

Source: © 2023 by Claudia Bertolone-Smith and Marlene Moyer. Used with permission.
Visit **go.SolutionTree.com/behavior** to download a free, full-color reproducible version of this figure.

Authors Daniel Siegel and Tina Payne Bryson (2020) discuss this idea in their book, *The Power of Showing Up: How Parental Presence Shapes Who Our Kids Become and How Their Brains Get Wired.* They emphasize that under normal circumstances, students should be in the green zone. This is when students are not under stress but can focus and be present with the tasks at hand. This is similar to the ability to be serious, assertive, and working. Siegel and Payne Bryson (2020) also highlight the red zone (orange for TNR), in which students' brains are too revved up due to emotions like fear and anger. With Tools Not Rules, we use the words *showboating, stuck,* and *aggressive* to indicate the revved-up zone.

Sometimes, students shut down, freeze, or hide. Students in this situation may put their head on their desk and not respond. A student may pull their hood over their head and face, with a clear message of not wanting to engage. In Tools Not Rules, these words are blue (*shirking, stuck, passive*). The colors can help teachers and students identify the quality of their behaviors more easily.

For example, if you ask a student to identify where they think they are in the Tools Not Rules language triads, and they can't identify a word, they may be able to identify a color. You might say, "Do you feel like you are in the blue zone or the orange zone?" Students often relate to this and can share the color related to what they are feeling. If a student identifies they are in the orange zone, you might say, "Thank you for your honesty about being in the orange zone. Do you think you are showboating? Do you feel stuck? Are you angry or feeling aggressive?"

> **Stop & Think**
>
> Review the word triads in figure 3.1 (page 53).
> When you are not in the green zone,
> how do you tend to react? Are you often hot-headed,
> over-involved, or looking for attention (orange)?
> Do you pull back when things get challenging or go quiet (blue)? Once you have identified your tendency, think about what helps you shift back to green. What strategies do you use?

Most people have a natural tendency to go to either the shut-down blue or the chaotic orange zone when they are dysregulated (Siegal & Payne Bryson, 2020). It's beneficial to understand your own reactions so when you have conversations with students, you are aware of how this might be influencing your emotions about the situation. Socrates, the ancient Greek philosopher, said, "Know thyself"—this holds great relevance and importance.

In the book *Building Resilience in Students Impacted by Adverse Childhood Experiences: A Whole-Staff Approach*, authors Victoria Romero, Richard Robertson, and Amber Warner (2018) make the important connection to understanding our own triggers and how this can support teacher well-being. Specifically, they remind us:

> Different events can trigger different responses in each one of us. We all have a past; humble yourself and embrace yours rather than try to deny it or run from it. By acknowledging

> and being mindful of our own triggers, they lose their power over us and we can develop self-care practices to keep us at our optimal best. (p. 22)

The language we use in Tools Not Rules provides a framework for us to practice self-awareness and management. Understanding your reactions to challenging learning or even life situations can help determine if your behaviors are getting in the way. If they are, then you can practice choosing something different and see if the situation resolves itself in a more positive way. When addressing student behaviors, especially those that trigger us, we must recognize our own emotions and psychological states and practice strategies to calm ourselves so we can be of service to students (Romero et al., 2018). Understanding that certain behaviors are making challenges even more complicated can be the first step in making indelible change.

The Logic Behind the Three Triads

After ten years of co-teaching in elementary school, we moved to the middle school level. There, we added the word triad *stuck, serious, silly*, as we noticed that when the work started getting harder, students often released pressure by making fun of things (*silly*) or sitting as if in cement, unable to move (*stuck*). Those who hadn't given up on themselves would ask questions or look for someone to help them (*serious*). This mirrors what Peter Liljedhal (2021), author of *Building Thinking Classrooms in Mathematics, Grades K–12: 14 Teaching Practices for Enhancing Learning*, finds in his research on what students do when trying what they have learned that day in independent work. He observes that most students engage in "mimicking, faking, slacking, and stalling," while few actually try the work (Liljedhal, 2021, p. 10).

We also found that at the middle school level, a new layer of behaviors emerged. Students often exhibited overt and covert anger that is regularly expressed at this age. So, we added the word triad *passive, assertive*, and *aggressive*. Students expressed aggression by shouting angry words or starting a fight. However, they also expressed anger in less obvious ways, such as stubbornness with underlying frustration: "I won't do what you ask." Students might also exhibit passive-aggressive behavior. A student might throw their hands in the air and exclaim, "You never gave me a paper!" This approach illustrates underlying anger directed at the teacher. In these incidents, we address the situation by beginning a conversation to see what the student is feeling.

We ask the student to be honest and then thank them for their honesty. We want students to know they matter. When they know they matter, they usually ask questions or get what they need to be successful (*assertive*).

These three triads of nine words encompass myriads of behaviors we observe, whether we are teaching at the elementary school, middle school, or university level. This approach doesn't overburden students with too many words. The learner can find their behavior somewhere in the triads and work toward becoming serious, assertive workers.

Some teachers wonder if they can change the list to better meet their needs. Absolutely, *yes*! You may find that other words work for your students or that using one triad might work well for your class. We encourage you to play with the language. While we have not attempted to adapt the full Tools Not Rules approach to a high school context, we can envision teachers engaging in similar adjustments that are more appropriate for grades 9–12 students. For example, when working with a high school, we changed *silly* to *sarcastic* to better address the older students' sensibilities. However, if you choose other words, we recommend keeping them to a manageable number so students can quickly recall what they mean and how they connect to their behavior. This makes behaviors shift quickly and keeps the classroom learning moving forward.

Common Language in the Classroom and Across the School

It is powerful when a school agrees to use common language about target behaviors and goals. In the article, "The Power of Common Language," authors Vanessa Scanfeld, LaShonda Davis, Leah Weintraub, and Vincent Dotoli (2018) discuss using different words in each grade level for behavior expectations and developing character. The difference in language each school year may confuse students about what is expected when they move to the next grade level, and needing to relearn expectations can prevent behavioral growth from flourishing from one year to the next. Using a common language is an important time saver, making sure teachers do not lose precious learning opportunities. When students experience consistency from class to class, even from school to school, they can hit the ground running when concepts, language, and terminology remain consistent (Scanfeld et al., 2018).

When teachers and administrators work together across the school, common language can create powerful shifts in communication and behavior. Following is a scenario that took place in Marlene's classroom. In this situation, using the common language and approach of Tools Not Rules, the administrator and teacher were able to resolve a difficult situation while maintaining a positive and connected relationship with the student.

> The start of the 2020–2021 year was different from any other. Not only were we coming back from COVID-19 stay-at-home orders, but the entire town was evacuated the first two weeks of school because a wildfire had burned to our community's front door. Students were dazed and confused. One thing we couldn't have anticipated was a TikTok challenge that was circulating among all students in the nation, including our middle school. The challenge was titled Devious Lick and encouraged students to film themselves stealing things or vandalizing their school. Soon, stories on the news showed schools with bathroom doors ripped off their hinges, and everything from bathroom soap dispensers to exit signs and fire extinguishers were disappearing. So, on the first day of school, some students were considering their own devious lick, including one of my students, David.
>
> As I do with all first days, I start weaving in conversations around our common Tools Not Rules language. If I can get students to start seeing they can be honest and vulnerable on the first day, then I can change behaviors much more quickly. I shared how I hated reading when I was their age because I couldn't concentrate. "Who feels the same?" An unnerving number of hands shot up. I shared that I never completed a book until I was twenty years old, even in advanced English classes. I talked about how brains are wired differently, and some people just have brains that make reading and writing more difficult than others, or our home lives complicate things.
>
> "Who feels like they have a brain like this?" I asked. Several hands waved in the air. Students quickly figured out that this was a place where they could tell the truth without being judged. Yet, even with all those positives, I knew this year was going to be tough.
>
> By the end of my second day, I was tired and dismayed when a student told me, "Some boys were by your desk yesterday, and one stole from you." On the first day of school! I was stunned. I asked who it was in the sea of faces that was rushing out the door. She said she didn't know who it was nor what he stole.
>
> The next day, I stood next to the Tools Not Rules posters and talked earnestly to my class. Again, I tried to remove shame and extol the virtues of honesty. I told them I knew that someone stole something from me and asked, "Who has heard of devious licks?" Most students raised their hands. "Who has ever stolen something?" Many admitted to this, including me. I thanked students for their honesty and told them I wasn't going to lecture, but I also told them that there is power in being honest.

Although we are not our behavior, our behavior can land us in hot water, and it is important to be real about it. I concluded by saying that if anyone knew anything about devious licks, they should email me or talk to me after class. Thankfully, a student pointed to the desk of the boy who stole from me. It was David, who came to class late each day, letting us all know he had arrived. His fist bumps and head nods let everyone know he thought he was in charge. It was disrespectful and brash.

I called my assistant principal, Juan. Juan is an amazing administrator who understood Tools Not Rules the first time Claudia and I presented it to him. He is a big-hearted, realistic person who supports teachers and students in the front office. I told him, "Juan, I know who stole something off my desk. It was David Moreno." Juan said he had it handled, and I knew he did. Accountability without shame. Juan called me after school and said, "Check this out. I called in David. As soon as he arrived, I stood up next to the Tools Not Rules posters and said, 'David, what do we value more than anything?' He opened right up. 'Mr. H, I stole a plastic drum off Ms. Moyer's desk. I feel terrible about it. I know where it is, and I will bring it back to her tomorrow and apologize. I will accept any punishment you feel I deserve.' That was it." Juan wrapped up the conversation by saying, "Marlene, this stuff works!" From there, we were able to agree on an act of accountability that was acceptable to all.

Reflecting on this event, I can't help but think about the power of many people at one school using a common language. David had heard my brief introductions to the language on the first few days of school, and some of his other sixth-grade teachers had used it also. Juan knew it well, too, and used a conversation about accountability without shame. That, coupled with David's courage, allowed for something magical to transpire.

The Value of a Predictable Approach

Teachers also benefit from the improvement in behavior and academic achievement Tools Not Rules can bring to their classrooms. This is directly related to the predictability of the approach. When behavior becomes difficult in the classroom, teachers can be caught off guard and need to find a quick way to respond. Often, their own history of reactions and emotions can get in the way. They might find themselves shouting or becoming irritated at students or retreating into silence and feeling frozen, not knowing how to respond. A seventh grader told us that one of her teachers ignores her doing gymnastics moves in her science classroom "because he doesn't know what to do with me."

When a teacher has a plan to address classroom behaviors, it creates a sense of calm in a tense moment. It provides predictability for both teachers and students. For the teacher, it may embolden or tame knee-jerk responses like yelling, avoiding, or ignoring. Students will see the teacher approach behaviors consistently. There are great benefits to this because students see that the teacher wants everyone to succeed, as every student is entitled to discussing their behavior and choosing a different one.

Review figure 1.2 in chapter 1 (page 22). It shows the TNR predictable approach.

1. First, we need to notice when a student is disengaged from learning. Disengagement can come in various forms, such as the following.
    a. A student should be doing group work, but they are not participating or are distracting other group members.
    b. A student should be silently reading, and instead, they are drawing.
    c. The class is listening to the teacher, but a student is blurting out ideas without raising their hand.
    d. A student should be engaging in a discussion, but they are using a rude tone with you or others.
2. After you notice the disengagement, quickly work to get the student back on track by doing the following.
    a. Ask the disengaged student to self-assess using the TNR language. For example, "Take a look at the posters. Where is your behavior right now? In the blue or the orange?"
    b. Allow the student to honestly tell you what is going on. Thank them for their honesty.
    c. Ask how they could get into the green areas (working, serious, assertive). Brainstorm things the student could do to get there.
    d. Once the student returns to work, notice small or big things they did to change their behavior and praise them for it. You can give them a discreet thumbs-up or mouth, "I see you being serious."

Teachers know that behavior issues are reoccurring, so this strategy helps them be ready for the next time or the next student. When you approach behavior with predictability, students learn that you will not overreact or underreact but will be clear and follow through with a pattern they have seen modeled in your classroom time and time again. Predictability builds a sense of emotional safety, something many students lack. They begin to trust that they will not experience the excruciating feelings that come with shame but instead will experience genuine regard, dignity, and effective help.

Tools Not Rules can be the first line of defense in fostering an effective learning environment. By having conversations with students using the TNR language, you can quickly get to the heart of what is causing student behavior shifts between the smaller behaviors and larger underlying concerns. When you recognize that there are bigger problems or issues for students (for example, constant anxiety or panic attacks, difficult situations at home, possible drug use, or depression), you can enlist the help of counselors to help support students' long-term health and wellness. Overall, using TNR to engage in honest conversations with students allows for immediate improvements in the classroom, while broadening the net of support when needed.

Tools Not Rules Language to Support Schoolwide Programs

Many schools implement school- or districtwide initiatives that focus on developing greater success in the classroom and life. For example, programs such as positive behavior interventions and supports (PBIS) encourage staff and students to make videos to help promote safe processes and procedures, such as how to walk safely in the hallways. These procedures are an effective piece to creating a safe and respectful campus. Other programs, such as EPIC (Empower, Prepare, Inspire, Connect) Learning (Douglas County School District, n.d.) ask teachers to identify and establish class codes for their individual classrooms. In some ways, these are a modern take on the old-fashioned classroom rules. They might read like this: *We will be ready to learn by having our materials on our desks. We will respect others and expect the same in return.* The focus of these programs includes the need to agree on rules and procedures that all students and staff can follow.

In *The New Art and Science of Teaching*, Marzano (2017) quantifies the top forty-three elements needed to be an effective teacher. Element 36 states that to be successful, teachers must acknowledge the adherence to rules and procedures. Conversely, element 37 states that instructors must acknowledge a lack of adherence to rules and procedures. He goes on to note that "such acknowledgement should not come in the form of punishment" (p. 85). Teachers put in tremendous effort helping students "adhere" to the rules and creating a successful system to acknowledge the lack of adherence to rules and procedures, especially to avoid punishment. Having rules and behavior norms are essential, but just telling students the rules or showing them behavior videos is not enough. These actions are important, but when used in isolation, they do not create compliance for many students.

Compounding this issue is the fact that fewer and fewer disrespectful and defiant classroom behaviors qualify for suspension (punishment). Not only do schools get low statewide marks for having high suspension rates, but strict laws prohibit large swaths of suspensions. For example, by 2020 in California, most public schools could no longer suspend students for willful defiance due to significant statistics showing racial bias (Suspensions and expulsions: willful defiance: interventions and supports, 2023).

According to Taylor Swaak (2019), the Los Angeles Unified School District (LAUSD) had not been suspending students for defiance since 2013. Suspensions for student defiance dropped from 17,595 students in the 2011–2012 school year to just 2,796 in 2017–2018. LAUSD found that historically marginalized students (who are often suspended at higher rates) were staying in school, which increased academic success and high school graduation (Swaak, 2019). However, advocates for this shift argue that banning suspensions is just the first step. There also needs to be a culture shift allowing for de-escalation, positive interventions, and a focus on restorative justice practices.

Tools Not Rules can take schoolwide discipline approaches like PBIS one step further, as TNR conversations do more than remind students about being safe, respectable, and responsible. The conversations are focused on self-awareness to help students identify the characteristics of their behavior. It moves to self-management by asking students to choose an action that will help them move to the "green zone" and toward serious, assertive, and working. This personalized micro-adjustment builds a foundation for increased moments of expected behavior and deeper teacher-student connection. Schoolwide discipline policies provide clear definitions of expected student behaviors, and the Tools Not Rules language and approach effectively develop students' ability to meet these standards.

Increased Engagement

Students know that some teachers will start teaching once they get to about 80 percent class engagement, meaning there is about 20 percent of the class who remain disengaged. When we have about 80 percent of students with us, the metaphorical

Adopting the Tools Not Rules Language

teaching bus often leaves the station. Once, a superintendent visiting our classroom summed this up by stating, "At some point, the ship must depart, whether you have everyone on board or not."

Getting 100 percent engagement in the classroom can be a struggle. We started this journey because we were frustrated when we couldn't engage all students at once. We felt that leaving the station before everyone was on board didn't make those who missed the boat feel compelled to pay attention. Instead, those who were not engaged did not know how to start their work. This increased the shirking, passive, and silly behaviors that disrupted the students who wanted to work. They were doing a myriad of things—texting under the table, tossing notes across the classroom, trying to get candy from their neighbor, sharpening their pencil, or asking to go to the bathroom. Eventually, to correct the balance between working and shirking, we ended up providing mini-reteach sessions to those who were left behind. Unfortunately, this prevented us from helping students who truly needed support and sent the message to students that participating in the lesson was optional.

Instead, we decided to focus on ensuring that *everyone* was ready to start and stay engaged during instructional time. We recognized that a large part of being serious, assertive, and working is learning to pay attention. Learning to pay attention is also about getting ready to receive information. In our quest for this goal, a few activities worked to get students' attention and sustain engagement. One thing we quickly learned is that we had to model, practice, and support students in paying attention. The 20 percent who were used to being left behind were surprised, as they preferred the status quo. The showboating students who were used to not having to pay attention because they "already knew how to do it" felt indignant.

If a student willfully refused to give us their attention, we had a private Tools Not Rules conversation to find out what was going on and sometimes put them on a star chart (see chapter 5, page 95). At first, we had to dig in to get undivided attention. Then, as students felt more competent and successful in their schoolwork, it became part of the classroom culture. In an odd turn of events, they were proud of themselves for being able to fully engage, and they expected it of each other. The following are the two strategies we use to engage students during instruction.

1. **Eyes and hands:** Try this when you need students to listen to you for no more than thirty seconds to clarify an idea, give directions, and so on.
    a. Everyone turns and twists their body to face you. There is nothing in their hands.

    b. You need everyone with you. Tell students, "Amazing, I have eighteen out of twenty-six. Now, there are twenty-two students ready. I am only waiting on two. Everyone matters to me, so I will wait." And you do—you wait until every student is paying attention.

    c. If someone is being stubborn and won't attend, then move to the cycle shown in figure 1.2 (page 22).

2. **Give me twenty-five:** When you need everyone's undivided attention for a minute or more, say, "Give me twenty-five!" When a student "gives you twenty-five," they are embodying attention with ten fingers, ten toes, two ears, two eyes, and one mouth, all pointing toward you. Make sure students' chairs are facing toward you, with the back of the chair behind them. Modeling this for students is helpful.

    a. Say, "Everyone, give me twenty-five!" At this prompt, students turn their chairs so their whole body is facing toward you and the back of the chair is behind them. This takes a moment, but don't skip it.

    b. Ask students to show you ten fingers, with nothing in their hands, ten toes pointing toward you on the ground, two ears listening, two eyes looking at you, and one closed mouth. That equals twenty-five. You will usually have to wait for a few students. "I have twenty of you, amazing. I have twenty-four, awesome. I am only waiting on one person. Great, we are ready to go!"

    c. Avoid using names to point out those who aren't ready yet, and see how this changes students' willingness to join in. Make sure students do not shout at those still figuring it out, as this causes embarrassment. Be sure that everyone is just quietly waiting. You are in charge of this.

    d. Letting students know you are waiting and that you care is helpful. "I support everyone here and everyone matters, so I will wait."

    e. You can try turning your back to students and slowly counting to ten while they make all the adjustments needed to give you their full attention. When you turn around, note if you are still waiting for some. "I am only waiting on four people to make micro-adjustments. Three people have things in their hands. Two people need to adjust their chairs."

f. Once you have their attention, ask students to put their hands in their lap and roll their shoulders back. You want them to relax and listen.

Asking for and getting twenty-five from students requires you to stick with it and wait. It is not for the faint of heart; but if you can follow through, you will ensure that all students know what is happening and what is expected to learn what you are teaching. You will waste less time repeating yourself and be less frustrated as more students become serious, assertive, and working.

Conclusion

One of the main reasons we use Tools Not Rules is to help students who keep themselves on the fringe and are at great risk of academic failure. We wanted to wake them up and call them in, using something new and different. The common language, predictability, and dogged determination work! Ultimately, Tools Not Rules language can keep you from giving up on resistant students. It helps you to continue seeking pathways to create new, successful experiences for students so they can see more of their potential.

In this chapter, we defined the Tools Not Rules language, the specific words we use to help students identify and change their behavior. We looked at the benefits to students and teachers of having classrooms with clearly defined common language. Additionally, we noted the power of having a whole school use common behavior language that everyone knows. When the administration works with the same language, it means you are all on the same page and meet students with a united front. You can hold students accountable and return to the classroom as soon as possible. Lastly, we discussed how this process-oriented approach to behavior will enhance other schoolwide or districtwide initiatives.

In the next chapter, we share how to teach Tools Not Rules language to students, along with a host of activities that help students understand what the Tools Not Rules language triads mean. These activities show students how you, the teacher, can use the language to help them become serious, assertive, and working.

Try This!

In this chapter, we discussed that being aware of our triggers and developing self-calming strategies are essential for both student and teacher well-being. Think of a student you work with now who triggers you. You may feel frustrated by their repeated behavior or find yourself complaining about this student often.

Take a moment to breathe deeply to help ease your frustration. You may wish to try square breathing, where you trace a square and breathe in the following pattern: Breath in for a count of five, hold your breath for a count of five, release your breath for a count of five, and hold your breath for a count of five. As you repeat breathing around the square, feel your body calm. Bring this student to mind and consider the following.

1. What triggers me about this student's behavior?
2. What does it remind me of? What happened to me that makes me so upset when this behavior occurs?

If you connect to what this is, remind yourself that the student is not purposely trying to trigger you. The student is acting out for another reason. Consider the following:

1. What does this student need or want that they are not getting in my classroom?
2. What could be at the root of their behavior? Is it trauma? Past poor experiences in school? Lack of ability? Are they embarrassed?
3. How can I connect with this student to understand more about what is happening and why?
4. How can I use this information to change the dynamic so the student no longer needs the behavior?

Try a non-triggered conversation with the student at a time when they are not exhibiting any negative or triggering behaviors. Create a space inside you where you are calm and taking care of yourself. Talk with the student to discover what might be going on. Practice the art of breathing, being open to the information, and possibly creating a solution. See how it goes!

Chapter 4

Teaching and Using the Tools Not Rules Language With Students

> *Tools Not Rules turns students ON instead of OFF. They engage in classroom learning and my connection with them. When I feel myself going to negative patterns, like using names, I switch to TNR and immediately feel a change in the climate. Students reengage. They start helping each other modify behaviors instead of me having to do all the work.*
>
> **M. Rios**, teacher, grade 6 ELA and ELD, personal communication, December 1, 2023

One of the first steps in using Tools Not Rules with students is to teach them what the words in the three language triads mean in your classroom. For example, *working* in an ELA classroom might involve quiet work or reading, while in a physical education class, it might involve rigorous engagement in games or fitness activities. We recommend teaching much more than the definition of the words; teach them in *context*.

When working with students, we teach them the *embodiment* of the words. For example, if we are discussing what *shirking* means in the classroom, we challenge students to envision how it looks, sounds, and feels, and the possible motivation for choosing this behavior. We talk about why honesty above everything is expected and how honesty is a powerful tool to use in life. This process also allows students to accurately use the words to self-assess and self-regulate. It provides a clear road map of how you, the teacher, will help everyone be successful.

In this chapter, we discuss how to use the Tools Not Rules language in the classroom and why the common language of Tools Not Rules helps you be consistent and effective in coaching students to become serious, assertive learners. The first part of this chapter is about teaching students the Tools Not Rules language. We share the importance of using the word *we* as you engage in teaching the language. Then, we highlight several activities we use to teach students what the words mean in the context of learning by providing a two- to three-week plan for quick, engaging, and fun lessons to help reinforce the language. Finally, we explore how to use the Tools Not Rules language to guide self-assessment and self-regulation while you teach and when students are working in class.

How to Teach Students the Tools Not Rules Language

You can teach students the Tools Not Rules language at any point in the school year; however, if you are able, starting during the first two weeks of a school year or semester is ideal. We start teaching the language on the first day of school. We want students to know right away that this is a different type of classroom, one where we *want* to hear the truth about who they are and how they experience school. We share stories about our challenges in school and ask students to raise their hands if they have ever felt the same. For example, you might share, "I hated reading when I was your age. I never finished a book. Who here feels the same about reading?" Hands fly up! You motion toward the posters and say, "In this classroom, we want honesty about *everything*. You can be honest with me." This is helpful groundwork for the next step—getting students to self-assess and self-regulate using the Tools Not Rules language.

As mentioned previously, make sure to post the Tools Not Rules language in your classroom where students can see it (see chapter 1, figure I.1, page 8). Remember, you can make the posters yourself (see figure 4.1), or you can order posters through our website (visit www.toolsnotrules.com). Some teachers post a small set of posters in the hallway outside their classroom door so students can self-assess when having a

Teaching and Using the Tools Not Rules Language With Students 69

conversation with the teacher about their behavior. Dual immersion programs have translated the posters to Spanish to use in their learning environments as well (see figure 4.2).

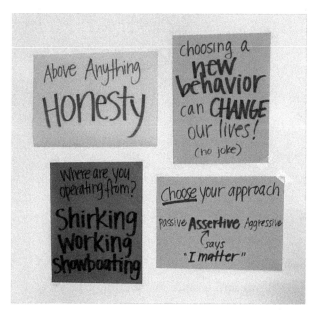

Source: © 2017 by Marlene Moyer. Used with permission.

FIGURE 4.1: Handmade Tools Not Rules posters.

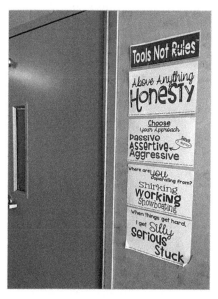

Source: © 2020 by Claudia Bertolone-Smith and Marlene Moyer. Used with permission

FIGURE 4.2: Small set of Tools Not Rules posters by the classroom door for one-on-one student conversations (left). Spanish version of the posters to use in dual immersion classrooms (right).

The posters are essential because you will use them to cue students to self-assess and self-regulate. Students see the words (as well as the colors blue, green, and orange), which helps them know what the goal is: serious, assertive, and working. Once the posters are up in your classroom, we suggest you start using the language right away. Whenever you are describing student behavior, practice fitting it into the language triads. As students hear and see the Tools Not Rules language, they will start connecting the words to what they mean.

The following are some ways you can do this.

- In emails to students or parents:
    - "Thank you for being assertive by writing to me. Awesome!"
    - "Connor was working and serious today when we did our social studies project."
    - "I appreciate your honesty about the situation."
- In quick one-on-one conversations:
    - "I see that you are working and serious. Wonderful!"
    - "I appreciate you being assertive in your group and taking notes."
    - "Thank you for shifting your behavior from silly to serious during our work time. It really made a difference in how much you accomplished."
- In praise for students hitting target behaviors:
    - "Thank you for being assertive and letting me know you forgot your book."
    - "Four of the groups in this class are already working—great job!"
    - "Thank you for letting me know where you were stuck on this problem. I can see you are now working on finishing it. Great job."
- In teacher-parent conferences or student study teams:
    - "Megan is really assertive during language arts; she always lets me know when she needs help."
    - "I notice that when Joey is shirking, it is usually because he needs more supplies and information to get started. I began checking in with him right away and noticed when he was working. This has helped."

Teaching and Using the Tools Not Rules Language With Students

An essential part of laying the foundation for using Tools Not Rules in your classroom is spending time helping students understand the approach. We call this *setting the stage* so students are aware of how you will help them learn and be successful in your classroom.

How to Set the Stage

Before we engage in any activities, we remind students that we will be honest when talking about the language. As mentioned previously, the most powerful use of this language is having students reflect on what the behaviors look like and why they might choose behaviors in the triads. This is an important point about engaging in these activities with students.

Consider the following scenario: Ms. Solares asks why students might be shirking in her social studies class. Note that we emphasized the use of the pronoun *we* instead of *you*.

Frankie:
We are shirking because social studies is boring.
(Other students laugh and agree.)

Ms. Solares:
What about it is boring? Be more specific.
Why are *we* bored?

Frankie:
Well, I don't know, there is a lot of reading, and *we* might not be great at reading.

Ms. Solares:
So, *we* might be shirking because *we* don't like to do so much reading?

continued →

Frankie:
Yes.

Ms. Solares:
Thank you for being honest, Frankie. What else? Why else might *we* be shirking?

Ms. Solares's inquiry for more information in this conversation conveys that blaming boredom for the reason why students choose shirking behaviors is only part of the story. She supports the students in further analysis and avoids reacting to the comments negatively. Instead, she pushes for more information. A student might be shirking by blaming others for why they can't do something ("It's boring") and resisting help and not wanting to try ("Because it is hard"). Students can practice self-assessment by wondering what else might be causing this behavior. The Tools Not Rules language activity is not meant to be an arena where students tear down the importance of practicing autonomy, agency, and competence in the school setting. Ms. Solares maintains the integrity of the situation and avoids shaming while allowing Frankie to share more.

The Importance of *We*

As you introduce the Tools Not Rules language to students, *we* is a very important word. We talked about the perspective that students are not their behavior and how helpful this is in freeing them up to choose something different. Each language triad consists of a range of behaviors that students might choose at any time during the school day. For example, if a student loves and is good at reading, they might be working and serious the entire time during language arts lessons. However, this same student might experience more of a challenge in mathematics, making it difficult to learn. During mathematics time, new behaviors might arise because the student is unsure and worried about being able to do the work.

This is why we tell students to use the word *we* when engaging in Tools Not Rules activities. For example, when introducing the triad *shirking, working,* and *showboating*, you might ask two important questions:

Teaching and Using the Tools Not Rules Language With Students

- "What does it look like when *we* are shirking?"
- "Why might *we* be shirking?"

The first question addresses what *shirking* looks like and what behaviors we are talking about when we use that word in the classroom. The second asks students to develop empathy and a deeper understanding of what a student may be feeling when they are shirking. It is tempting for students to respond with, "Some people are shirking because they don't listen during class," or "I don't do this, but some people just avoid the work by acting like they are tired and putting their heads down on the desk." Both statements weaponize the situation, and the conversation can disintegrate into negativity and accusations. It can also instigate "othering," such as, "I don't do this, but others in the class do." This type of language is loaded with shame and must be avoided.

We have found that asking students to share what shirking looks like goes well when helping them avoid tattling on others' behaviors. We let students know that the discussion is about the whole class, not an individual student, and this makes a difference. When doing this activity, we keep asking, "What does it look like when we are shirking? What are we doing in class? What else are we doing?" The following are some examples of how students might respond.

- "When we sharpen our pencil instead of getting started on our work."
- "We lose our worksheet, so we don't have to do the work."
- "We ask to go to the nurse so we can get out of the assignment."
- "We talk to our partners and try to distract them."
- "We say we don't get it or that it is too easy."

During this activity, if a student forgets about using the word *we* and instead, uses *some people*, we gently remind them to say it again, using *we*. Because *we* are human, the truth is that each one of us might find ourselves shirking or showboating at times. The goal is to create a comprehensive and honest list of shirking behaviors—one that does not cast blame but is a depersonalized view of what happens in the classroom.

During our Tools Not Rules study (see the appendix, page 131), one gifted student shared that he was always working and ahead in his classes until eighth grade when science became more complicated. He found himself shirking—not doing the work, making excuses, not asking questions, and lying about homework. He reflected that the Tools Not Rules language and in-class conversations helped him understand what was happening. He understood he was shirking because, for the first time, he needed to pay more attention in class, ask for support, and work harder on assignments.

He was grateful for this insight and ability to shift his behavior. Tools Not Rules provides a framework for self-reflection that can prompt students to positively change their approach at any time to get different results.

Simple Activities for Teaching Tools Not Rules Language

Engaging, inclusive activities are a great way to introduce the Tools Not Rules language triads. This section offers activities you can use to teach the TNR language to students. We share examples of how you might teach the triad *shirking-working-showboating* in our examples. You can use the same activities for the triads of *stuck-serious-silly* and *passive-assertive-aggressive* as well. (To find additional activities visit **go.Solution Tree.com/behavior**.)

Sharing Stories

For this activity, provide a clear definition of the word (for example, *shirking*), and then ask students to share in small groups about a time when they might have exhibited this behavior. For example, the prompt for *shirking* might be:

Think of a time when you didn't want to do something you needed to do, and you wanted to avoid it. What did you do? Share at your table or with a shoulder partner. Come up with three examples of how we avoid things we don't like or don't want to do.

Playing Charades: Are You Shirking, Working, or Showboating?

Everyone loves a good skit! To play charades with the TNR words, print and cut apart slips of paper featuring the words you are discussing, such as *shirking, working,* and *showboating*. Each group chooses a strip of paper and then plans a short skit showing what the behavior looks like in the classroom. You can have individual students guess or have groups write their answers on a whiteboard and then show them to the class. The group that performed the charade shares what they were acting out. Students really enjoy this activity, and it provides a formative assessment regarding their current understanding of the language, which is helpful as you proceed.

Describing What It Looks Like

Make a list of the words in the triad electronically (for example, a Google Slides or Google Doc) or on chart paper as an anchor chart, similar to figure 4.2 (page 69).

The goal is to have students identify what each word in the triad looks like when it is happening in class, as well as *why* the student might be exhibiting this behavior.

Consider team teaching this activity so one teacher can type or write and another can elicit responses. Try to get as many responses for each word as possible, as this helps cover a range of ideas and definitions.

Figure 4.3 and figure 4.4 show examples of student responses.

Shirking	Working	Showboating
Our heads are down on our desks.	We are looking at the teacher.	We say we already know the answer.
We ask to go to the nurse.	We have what we need.	We try to always finish first.
We lose our stuff for the class work.	We ask questions.	We tell everyone we are done.
We mess around with things.	We get started right away.	We say that the work is too easy.
We talk instead of work.	We help others.	We rush through the work.

FIGURE 4.3: What does the behavior look like?

Shirking	Working	Showboating
We don't want people to know we can't do it.	We want to do well in school.	We want the attention.
We think it makes people like us if we don't do the work.	We don't want to fail.	We want the teacher to know we already know how to do it.
We think it is too difficult.	We just want to get it done.	We are trying to get back at people who are mean.
We don't understand.	We like the topic.	We are mad that we are not in an advanced class.

FIGURE 4.4: Why might we be doing these behaviors?

Lifting Our Learning

One of our study participants moved from teaching middle school to first grade. When teaching her students about the triads, she asks, "What behaviors *lift* our ability to learn? What behaviors *weigh down* our ability to learn?" This allows younger students (grades K–3) to focus on two different types of behaviors in the classroom that impact learning. Along with the Tools Not Rules language, you can use this information to help coach and guide students to choose lifting behaviors as they learn.

This teacher posted anchor charts in her classroom to reference with students (see figure 4.5).

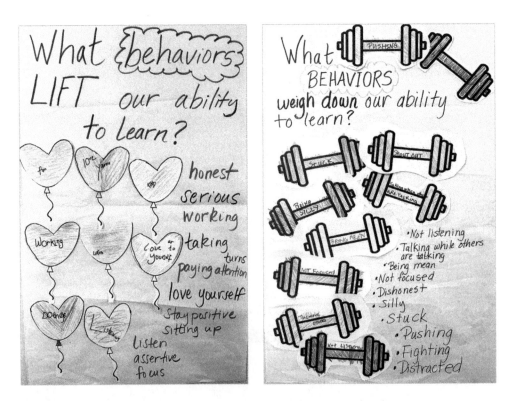

Source: © 2024 by Claudia Bertolone-Smith and Marlene Moyer. Used with permission.

FIGURE 4.5: What behaviors lift our ability to learn? What behaviors weigh down our ability to learn?

Modeling Individual Redirection

Students feel safe in their learning environment when they know what to expect and understand classroom routines. During this activity, act out with a student what happens when they are asked to self-assess and change their behavior.

Teaching and Using the Tools Not Rules Language With Students

1. Tell students, "We are going to look at how I can help you identify what's happening with your behavior, and then choose an action to move toward becoming serious, assertive, and working."

2. Ask a student to act out an orange or blue behavior. For example, "We need a volunteer to act out being passive in class."

3. As the student begins to act passive, demonstrate the following conversation. Walk to their desk, making sure the class can see and hear you while having this conversation.

    > *Teacher:* Hi, Jonah, look at the posters on the wall. Can you tell me where you are? What word describes how you feel or are acting?
    >
    > *Jonah:* Yeah, I'm being passive. I don't have my homework 'cause I left it at home. I'm bummed.
    >
    > *Teacher:* Thanks for being honest, Jonah. What is one thing you can do right now to be assertive?
    >
    > *Jonah:* Well, I think I can get started on the work and ask you if it is okay if I bring in my homework tomorrow.
    >
    > *Teacher:* That is really assertive. Yes, you can bring in your homework tomorrow. I'll make a note of it. Do you need my help getting started on the work?
    >
    > *Jonah:* No, I get how to do it.
    >
    > *Teacher:* Great, nice job being assertive.

Modeling Whole-Class Redirection

Tell students, "Let's look at how we can use the Tools Not Rules posters to help us make changes in our behavior." Ask them to pretend to start to work at their desks, showing orange, green, and blue behaviors.

Get students' attention and ensure everyone is looking at you. Then, follow these steps.

1. Tell students, "Everyone, look at the Tools Not Rules posters." Find the word that describes what behavior you are engaging in right now. Tell a neighbor. Where do you need to go? What can you do to get there? Thank you for your honesty."

2. Students turn and talk, and then get back to work.

As students share, most of them will reflect appropriately. You may have a few who insist they are working when they are not. Instead of calling them out in front of the whole class, have a one-on-one conversation using the Tools Not Rules approach, which we discuss in the following section. We encourage you to develop your own strategies to share the language and definitions with students, as we know educators are constantly thinking about new ways to teach content. As you work through the language triads, be sure to use the words while teaching and talking with students so they can see what they mean in context.

Setting the Standard

Another great strategy to use before students start independent or group work is to set the standard for what exactly *serious*, *assertive*, and *working* looks like during the activity or lesson. You can ask students to describe it, or you can say something like, "While we do our lab today in science, serious, assertive, and working means using the lab equipment the right way and working together to follow the procedures. Also, each student will fill in the lab sheet, and you can help others in your group."

This helps students to picture what you mean by serious, assertive, and working in the context of how they engage in the activity. It also helps them self-assess and self-regulate more accurately because they are aware of what you expect. As you develop and use the language, the key point is that, as human beings, we choose our behaviors and there are reasons why we choose them. But there are also consequences for those behaviors. Each of us can choose different behaviors to get different outcomes. As we grow, we have many opportunities to work on this. During the process of teaching and using the Tools Not Rules approach, take moments to discuss this as well.

A Plan for Rolling Out the Tools Not Rules Language

If you would like a more formal plan to follow, we offer a day-to-day rollout of activities to get your classroom started with Tools Not Rules. The activities ensure that students know what the language means and how you will use it in the classroom. You may want to complete one or more activities each day, or a few lessons each week for two to three weeks, after introducing the language. We use TNR language with students while we are completing the activities in the rollout, which helps students understand more fully when they see it in action. We usually begin the rollout on the first day of school, but it will work whenever you begin Tools Not Rules.

Teaching and Using the Tools Not Rules Language With Students

Figure 4.6 provides a sequential plan for teaching students about Tools Not Rules. For each activity, we provide the language focus and a brief description. We created a "Tools Not Rules Student Rollout" slideshow, which has premade slides you can use with your class for each activity. There are worksheets that go along with several of the lessons. (Visit www.toolsnotrules.com for free access to links and supporting materials.)

Activity and Time Needed	Tools Not Rules Language Focus and Description
Activity 1: Who has ever? (Five minutes)	**TNR Language:** *Honesty above anything.* **Description:** In this activity, students work on developing trust and honesty in the classroom. It helps students recognize the value of honesty in evaluating their own behaviors, which allows them to make important changes that work. Begin by asking students to raise their hand if they have ever engaged in certain behaviors. For example, you might ask, "Raise your hand if you have ever borrowed answers on a test because you didn't want to fail," or "Raise your hand if you've ever gotten so mad that you said something you regret." For younger students, you might ask, "Raise your hand if you have ever said something mean to a friend," or "Raise your hand if you have ever purposely left someone out at recess." Thank students for their honesty. Students will realize they are not the only ones who have made mistakes, and they learn that being honest helps them take responsibility for their choices. We never use students' responses to shame or tease them for what they do. We ensure that the conversation is not glorifying poor behavior choices; instead, it helps students learn about their ability and willingness to be honest. Visit www.toolsnotrules.com to see the full activity.
Activity 2: What raises your ability to learn? What lowers your ability to learn? (Fifteen to twenty minutes)	**TNR Language:** *You are not your behavior.* **Description:** To help students separate their behaviors from who they are, complete a poster similar to those shown in figure 4.5 (page 76). Students identify a behavior they have that brings their ability down (weight) and ability up (balloon). This can be useful for all ages through middle school but can be especially helpful for grades K–3.
Activity 3: Acting 101— Are you stuck, serious, or silly? (Five minutes)	**TNR Language:** *Stuck, serious, silly* **Description:** While sitting in their chairs, have students act out what it looks like when they are stuck, serious, or silly. What does it look like when we are stuck? What does it look like when we are serious? What does it look like when we are silly? Narrate as you observe different behaviors around the classroom. For example: "I see people doodling on their paper . . . some of us have our heads down . . . a few are trying to get their neighbor's attention . . . we look stuck!"

FIGURE 4.6: Lesson sequence for rolling out Tools Not Rules language in class.

continued →

Activity and Time Needed	Tools Not Rules Language Focus and Description
Activity 4: What does it look like? Why do we do it? (Ten to twenty minutes)	**TNR Language:** All triads **Description:** It can be liberating for students to tell the truth about what is happening at school. In this activity, students share what each behavior looks like and reflect on why they might choose this behavior. Collectively, the class fills out a table for each language triad. Class Behaviors: What do these behaviors look like? | Shirking | Working | Showboating | |---|---|---| | | | | | | | | | | | | | | | | Class Behaviors: Why do we do these behaviors? | Shirking | Working | Showboating | |---|---|---| | | | | | | | | | | | | | | | | This activity is important for building student empathy. Students have to use the word *we* when sharing their answers. Make sure to thank them for their honesty. Resist editing their responses or trying to talk them out of it. We have found great success when we thank them for being honest and putting their idea on the list. For the "Why do we do these behaviors?" chart, student responses may start at the surface level. A student may say, "We don't like reading," but it might move to statements such as, "We are afraid to look dumb," "We don't know what is going on," or "School has always been hard." Make sure to thank students for these honest statements. You may access the two charts at www.toolsnotrules.com.

Teaching and Using the Tools Not Rules Language With Students

Activity and Time Needed	Tools Not Rules Language Focus and Description
Activity 5: Comic strip (Twenty minutes)	**TNR Language:** *Shirking, working, showboating* **Description:** Students draw pictures in a three-box comic strip template to illustrate a complete language triad (for example, *shirking, working, showboating*). They can add dialogue to help show what someone might be saying while doing this behavior. You may give each student a different triad or have them choose which one they would like to illustrate. Cut and glue the finished product to a poster so students can refer to it throughout the year. You may access the comic strip student page at www.toolsnotrules.com.
Activity 6: When have you been passive, assertive, or aggressive? (Ten minutes)	**TNR Language:** *Passive, assertive, aggressive* **Description:** Describe to the class what each word in the triad means. If you feel comfortable, you might share an example of when you have exhibited these behaviors. Ask students to think of a time when they acted passive, and have them share with a partner. Walk around the room, listening to students' stories, and say, "I heard people share things like. . . ." This helps build students' understanding of what passive means and what might cause this behavior. Repeat this process for the words assertive and aggressive. Make sure to honor students' honesty for sharing. Resist correcting them or using sarcasm as they share. Thanking them for their honesty is appropriate here.
Activity 7: Charades (Twenty-five minutes)	**TNR Language:** All triads **Description:** Now that students are familiar with all three triads, you can play charades. In small groups, students draw a slip of paper from a box with a TNR word on it. Each group then plans a skit of the word to act out in front of the class. All other groups watch and guess the word. They can write their answers on a piece of paper or whiteboard to share with the class. Award points for correct answers. You may download the list of charade words from www.toolsnotrules.com.
Activity 8: Memes (Fifteen minutes)	**TNR Language:** All triads **Description:** Students love memes and using them is a great way to connect students to the meaning of the language triads. In this activity, students find memes online that illustrate specific Tools Not Rules words. They then insert their memes into the Meme Activity Worksheet, so others can see them and increase their understanding of the language. You may find the link to the digital Meme Activity Worksheet at www.toolsnotrules.com.
Activity 9: Practicing using the words (Ten minutes)	**TNR Language:** All triads **Description:** Model how you will use individual and whole-group interventions with students so they know what will happen in your classroom when using the Tools Not Rules approach.

continued →

Activity and Time Needed	Tools Not Rules Language Focus and Description
Activity 9: Practicing using the words (Ten minutes)	Tell students, "Let's look at how we can identify what's happening with our behavior and then choose an action to move towards becoming serious, assertive, and working. We need a volunteer to act out _____ (identify blue or orange behavior, such as *stuck*)." Have the student act out the word in their seat. Then, call them to the front of the class to model the individual intervention. Ask the student to look at the language triads and tell you which one describes their behavior. Then, ask them what green word they could choose instead (for example, serious, assertive, or working). Thank the student for their honesty and ask if there is anything you can do to help them change this behavior (Do they need a mentor? Do they need a pencil or other materials?). Act out helping the student get what they need and go back to their seat to start working. Next, try the activity as a whole group. Ask half of your students to act out blue or orange words, while the other half acts out green words. With your attention signal, ask them all to pause what they are doing, look at the Tools Not Rules word wall, and tell a neighbor what their current behavior is. Then, ask them to share what behavior they should move towards (green). Thank them for their honesty. Remember, this whole-group redirection should help refocus students quickly, so they can get back to work. There is no need to hear each student's plan or comment on the quality of their reflection.

Teachers in grades K–3 often wonder if it is difficult for younger students to understand these words and concepts. One first-grade teacher emphatically shared that her students can quickly grasp the language and the idea of separating their behavior from who they are. Her students created weights and balloon posters (see examples in figure 4.5, page 76) to model this idea. This quickly helped her students see behavior as a choice that can impact an outcome. Additionally, by using Google Slides, along with charades and acting out behaviors in their chairs, her students began using the words immediately. This teacher also used engaging call-and-response chants to help reinforce the concepts.

Teacher: *Let's not shirk . . .*

Students: *Let's work!*

Teacher: *We're not shirking!*

Students: *We're working!*

When asked if the words should be modified to easier ones for students in grades K–3, she emphatically replied, "No, they can do it!"

A New Way to Praise Students

Once students know the language triads, it's time to put them to work in your classroom. In this section, we first propose a change in how educators praise students. Then, we discuss approaches to individual and whole-class conversations using the Tools Not Rules language. As you read, see if you can picture how this change in approach might improve your relationship with students and preserve your positive teaching energy.

Teacher praise can have unintended consequences. Teachers may praise students for the outcomes of their work and attribute a personal characteristic to it, such as: "You are so smart. You got everything right on the worksheet!" or "Wow! You've read so many books already. You are an awesome reader!" According to Harvard University's Center on the Developing Child (n.d.), praising children for their intellect, skill level, or grades can foster a performance orientation. This motivates students to achieve rewards rather than challenge themselves in a learning environment, which can develop a fixed mindset (Dweck, 2016). As discussed in chapter 1 (page 17), a fixed mindset toward learning may limit a student's initiative to try new things, as they feel their knowledge level won't change.

This type of praise can also make one student happy, but interesting things might happen to the rest of the class. Some students might become distracted, trying to convince the teacher that they had completed the assignment early or had gotten everything correct. They might wonder why the teacher didn't notice *them*. And still, other students hear that you must have all correct answers to be noticed by the teacher, which can be defeating and might lead to shirking.

For those who didn't receive praise, the consequence can be feelings of shame or jealousy. Conversely, if we praise students for effort and persistence, they are more motivated to work hard and are "more likely to believe that they can achieve what they put their mind to" (Harvard Center for the Developing Child, n.d.). This can develop a growth mindset (Dweck, 2016), as discussed in chapter 1 (page 17), in which students willingly engage in productive struggle and can see that they are growing in their knowledge and ability.

As teachers, we must be aware of the power we hold to show students what is valued, who is valued, and what deserves praise. While co-teaching, we made a significant change to how we praised students, and we eventually called it *Magic, Fuzzy Numbers*. Here is what we did.

- **We stopped using students' names:** We stopped using names to correct individual students in front of the whole group (those who weren't ready, working, or paying attention). We did this because it created an inaccurate perception of what was happening in the class. It also began to impact our relationships with these students. We were using our teaching energy inefficiently, and we wanted this to change. So, we stopped calling out students as examples of appropriate behavior to get the class to do what we wanted. For example, when asking students to be ready on the carpet, we used to say, "I like the way Leilani is sitting criss-cross applesauce." This put an unnecessary focus on Leilani. The ultimate goal was for the whole class to get ready quickly and efficiently, so we weren't wasting valuable instructional time. Instead, we narrated the serious, assertive, and working behaviors we saw without using individual names. For example, "I see students sitting quietly. I love this!" or "I see 100 percent of the class facing the board. That shows you are ready to learn. Well done!"

- **We used Magic, Fuzzy, Numbers:** Because we wanted 100 percent engagement, we started using numbers to describe the serious, assertive, and working state of the class. For example, if we prompted, "Please take out your science journals and your calculator," we cruised the classroom and noticed how many students accomplished this request. We might check table groups and say, "Four out of six students in this group are ready to go—amazing!" When students made slight changes, we noted this too: "I just noticed three students who now have their calculators out. That's great!" The reason we use fuzzy numbers is because we are often estimating an accurate numerical value. We might say, "Eighty-six percent of us are ready to go; thank you for being serious about your learning!" The reason we call this magic is because it works incredibly well!

  If you have a few stubborn students, just check in with them later. Don't wait to get 100 percent engagement and be vigilant about not calling individual names. Just make a note to follow up, such as, "Hey, I noticed that . . . Do you know what behavior that is for you?" (Point to the TNR posters.) "If not, check out the blue or orange words. Can you tell me about that? Do you feel stubborn? Aggressive? Assertive?" Thank them for their honesty and see if anything shifts. If you see a change the next time you ask students to do something, make sure to privately acknowledge it: "I see you have all your science materials ready—that's awesome! Thank you for being serious about your learning."

- **We used student language to describe *working*:** We used the way students described *working* (see figure 4.3, page 75) to help them connect with what we expected. For example, when the class starts an assignment, we might say, "I see eleven people with their pencils ready, and I see two people already reading the first problem. According to the list we made, that is serious and working—great job!" When we experienced a moment when *everyone* was working, we might say, "One hundred percent of our class has the materials they need, and they are focusing on the problems they need to solve. I've also had three people ask good questions to help them understand, which is assertive. That is amazing. Keep up the serious, assertive work!" (If you have a whole-class reward system, this is a great time to use it!)

- **We increased happiness, engagement, and curiosity:** When we use Magic, Fuzzy Numbers, students are constantly curious. "Is it me? Am I part of the 12.5 percent that still needs to be ready?" or "Am I in the 84.7 percent who is on task?" Everyone in the class starts paying attention and making micro-adjustments as the group gets closer to 100 percent. Students who are off task wonder if they have been seen and then adjust their behaviors. This approach alleviates the power struggles that can often happen by creating a whole-class target goal void of shame. It generates an increasingly positive classroom environment because of the novelty of using numbers instead of names. Once we started using these strategies, we never went back. We were happier and less stressed in the classroom, and this increased our teaching energy.

The outcomes of using this type of praise are what *stopped* us from doing it. It helped us notice what wasn't working and how students reacted to us. For example:

- **We stopped calling out students who weren't ready, weren't working, or weren't paying attention:** We stopped praising students who made us feel acknowledged when they did what we asked, for example: "I really like the way Jenna is sitting criss-cross applesauce," which is really a passive-aggressive way to let Jenna know that rolling on the carpet during story time is not OK. This helped us separate students from their behaviors and take their behavior personally. Instead, we focused on what was going right and helped students understand what it looks like and feels like to work on something. So, we now praise serious, assertive, and working behaviors.

- **Students became engaged and curious:** Students are constantly guessing, "Is it me? Am I part of the 12.6 percent that still needs to be ready?" or "Am I in the 84.6 percent who is on task?" Everyone in the class starts paying attention and making micro-adjustments as the group gets closer to 100 percent. Students who are off task wonder if they have been seen and then adjust their behaviors. We also began praising individual students for making the adjustments needed to get to 100 percent, especially if it was a new move toward cooperation. The power of this single move feels like a classroom miracle! We were so much happier in the classroom and less stressed, and this increased our teaching energy.

Note that if you have a few students who are stubborn, just check in with them later. Don't wait forever to get 100 percent. Just make a note and follow up with a conversation to the side: "Hey, I noticed that . . . Do you know what behavior that is for you?" (Point to the TNR posters.) "If not, check out the blue or orange words. Can you tell me about that? Do you feel stubborn? Aggressive? Assertive?" Thank them for their honesty and see if anything shifts.

Stop & Think

How do you use praise in your classroom or when you are working with students? What results do you get when you are trying to adjust individual or whole-class behavior? Who gets praise in your classroom? Is there any bias in the ways you praise students?

Teaching and Using the Tools Not Rules Language With Students

There are several ways you can use Tools Not Rules to praise students in your classroom. This depends on what students need at the time. For example, if you want to acknowledge the whole class for serious work, you might use the Tools Not Rules language to frame what they are doing that meets the level of serious work. Or, if you see a student make a micro-adjustment after a personal conversation, you might use individual praise by clearly stating what the behaviors are that they chose (self-regulation) and how this meets the mark for serious, assertive, and working.

Figure 4.7 offers some examples of how to apply Tools Not Rules strategies for offering praise and correction in the classroom.

Praise for the Whole Group	**Magic Fuzzy Numbers** "Forty-two percent of us have our books out and are reading. Now, we have 65 percent. Awesome. Now, we have 92 percent. Great. This shows that we are serious, assertive, and working." **TNR Praise Language** "This silence tells me that students are serious, assertive, and working." "You've told me that serious, assertive, and working is having your supplies and starting right away. I see many of you doing this now—great job."
Praise for Individual Students	"I noticed that you got started right away today, and you have already completed five questions. That is assertive and working."
Correction for the Whole Group	"Everyone stop for a minute. Look at the posters and tell a neighbor what your behavior is right now. If you are not serious, assertive, and working, tell them what you need to do to get there. Thank you for your honesty."
Correction for Individual Students	"Hi, Ana. Thanks for talking to me. What do we love above anything?" "Honesty." "Okay, thank you. Can you look at the posters and tell me where your behavior is right now? What's really going on for you? Thank you so much for your honesty." (If needed, take some guesses as to what you think is going on, coming from a place of compassion.)

continued →

Conversation With an Individual to Learn More	"Can you step outside, please?" (We usually stand in the doorway so we can see the class as well as have a private conversation with the student.) "You know we value honesty above anything. I would love to know what is going on for you right now." "How can I help you? Is it something in class? At home? With friends? Thank you for your honesty."

FIGURE 4.7: Tools Not Rules strategies for praise and correction in the classroom.

Individual and Group Assessment

One of the key parts of Tools Not Rules is individual conversations with students and whole-class adjustments. In both situations, we are coaching students to honestly assess what is going on and actively choose an adjustment to their behavior if necessary. In this section, we describe how to smoothly run an individual and whole-group self-assessment to get students back on track.

Individual Self-Assessment

When using Tools Not Rules, it's important to distinguish between confession and self-assessment. We want a confession from a student when we ask, "Did you just throw this pencil across the room? You almost hit someone in the face!" We may be upset, concerned, and frustrated that this behavior has happened on our watch. What are they thinking? We are anxious to catch and distinguish the behavior, and perhaps move to a consequence.

Students cringe when asked to provide confessions in front of their peers, and while we don't mean to, we have potentially unloaded a heap of shame onto the student without fully knowing what really happened. Helping a student toward self-assessment is something quite different, and we can get both the confession and the consequence without shame. Remember to do this with a neutral tone of voice and from a stance of curiosity. Calm your own emotional reactions if you feel triggered. Don't take it personally. You are wondering and open. Move out of reaction and into listening.

You have a few choices when helping a student self-assess and identify how to change their behavior. See some examples of how Mr. Jefferson and Raul can engage in an individual discussion using the Tools Not Rules posters.

Teaching and Using the Tools Not Rules Language With Students

Example 1:

During science class, Mr. Jefferson notices that Raul is not taking notes but, instead, is flicking wads of paper at a friend. His friend starts yelling at Raul, and Mr. Jefferson asks Raul to come talk with him for a moment.

Mr. Jefferson:
Hey, Raul, tell me where you are with your behavior right now.

Raul looks at the posters to self-assess.

Raul:
Silly. I need to get serious.

Mr. Jefferson:
Do you need help with this?

Raul:
No.

Raul gets back to work.

Example 2:

Mr. Jefferson asks Raul to walk over to the posters to find out where he is and what behavior he can choose instead. Mr. Jefferson continues to work with other students. Raul then comes back to tell Mr. Jefferson what he has discovered about his behavior and what he should move toward. Mr. Jefferson thanks him for his honesty.

Example 3:

Mr. Jefferson asks Raul to talk with him for a moment. Raul's friend gets back to work.

continued →

Mr. Jefferson:
So, Raul, I want you to remember that I value honesty. That is what I'm looking for now. I see you throwing paper at your friend and not getting started on your work. What's going on for you?

Raul:
Yeah, I am throwing paper at him because he won't shut up. He keeps teasing me about something that happened after school yesterday. I want him to knock it off.

Mr. Jefferson:
Thank you for your honesty, Raul. We can have a conversation between you and your friend right after class. Would that work?

Raul:
Yeah.

Mr. Jefferson:
What do you need to get started on your science assignment?

Raul:
Nothing, but I don't want to sit by him right now.

Mr. Jefferson:
Okay, I'll move you over by the window. Can you get your stuff and start working?

Raul:
Yeah.

After class, Mr. Jefferson, Raul, and his friend discuss the issue.

Teaching and Using the Tools Not Rules Language With Students

In the following scenario, a second-grade teacher, Ms. Annecy, works with a small group while other students read silently in the classroom. She notices two students talking instead of reading. This scenario shows how Ms. Annecy uses the Tools Not Rules language to help students reflect on and shift their behavior.

Ms. Annecy is working at a table with a small group of students engaged in literacy instruction. Other students around the room are reading silently. Two students (Maia and Stuart) are talking instead of reading. Ms. Annecy leaves her desk and crouches to the floor with the students.

Ms. Annecy:
Hello, I am struggling to teach right now. Do you know why that might be? Can you tell me what your behavior is right now?

Maia:
We are being a bit silly.

Stuart:
I think I'm shirking because we are talking.

Ms. Annecy:
OK, thank you for being honest. What can you do instead?

Stuart:
We can get serious and read. And move. I can move.

Ms. Annecy:
Thank you for being honest and changing your behavior. I can see you both want to be serious about your reading.

In these scenarios, there was no need for further consequences because the students regulated their behavior. However, it is important to note that Tools Not Rules complements any school's rules and discipline procedures for students. Helping individual students be honest, identify their behavior, and self-regulate can increase their sense of autonomy (ability to choose another behavior), belonging (they matter to the teacher), and competency (as they choose different behaviors in the green zone, they start to feel what it is like to flourish). You are laying a strong foundation of connection with your students and your class, and even when there is a minor or major consequence, they know you are still committed to them and their learning.

Whole-Group Self-Assessment

Whole-group self-assessment is helpful when it feels like you have lost too many students in the group to redirect just a couple. The following group approach can quickly change the energy and get everyone back on track.

Mr. Jackson:
OK, everyone, stop. Look over the behavior choices on the TNR posters. Put your hand on top of your head once you know where your behavior is. Tell a neighbor. What do you need to do to get in the green?

Mr. Jackson listens to students' responses. He hears words such as *silly, stuck, shirking,* and *aggressive.* He knows many students are being honest, and he doesn't need to hear from specific students.

Mr. Jackson:
Thanks for your honesty; now get back to work.

Teaching and Using the Tools Not Rules Language With Students

This group adjustment works to get everyone more focused and moving forward. All students look at the posters and share them with each other. It is a chorus of answers. Immediately, they go back to focus on the task at hand. At this point, be sure to use Magic, Fuzzy Numbers to coach the whole class toward being serious, assertive, and working. It might sound something like this: "Right now, 67 percent of the class is focused on their writing. I see them rereading their work and making the edits they need. Five people just got their computers out and are logging on—great job! We are now at 84 percent of the class working. Oh! Four more people are now working—excellent! This is what it looks like to be serious, assertive, and working!"

If you do not get 100 percent of students working, begin individual conversations to see what students need to get started. Make sure to acknowledge small shifts from students who take the first steps toward working. It might sound like this: "I noticed that you have your computer and your book out on your desk. Thank you for being assertive and getting what you need to work."

Educators who provide quick, clear, and positive feedback when a student takes a step toward academic success or manage their behavior in a new way are "literally energizing the brain" (Romero et al., 2018, p. 64). When we interviewed students for our study, they reported that they liked the teacher checking in on them personally and individually. Some students shared that other teachers just say, "Get to work!," but Tools Not Rules teachers ask about *them*, which they found more effective and interesting. Several students mentioned that the Tools Not Rules language asked about them *personally*, which came across as respect and support from the teacher.

Conclusion

Students who are struggling with their classroom behavior might hear, "What are you doing? You need to get it together and get with the program!" They might not know what they are meant to be doing or what they need to get together, and furthermore, what program they should follow. One of the reasons Tools Not Rules is so effective is that it provides three simple triads for you to use when working with students and supporting them in self-assessment and self-management. We haven't met a student behavior that didn't fall into one of these categories.

Additionally, it gives students a way to communicate with you about what is going on ("I'm being silly") and predefined options for a new behavior ("I can shift to being serious"). When you ask students how they will make this shift, they learn to regulate themselves in the classroom. Tools Not Rules language eliminates confusion and helps the teacher and students experience clear, honest, and impactful communication. One of the teachers in our study shared that she "always had this in her heart," but she just didn't know how to say it. After implementing Tools Not Rules in her classroom, she would remind her students, "If you can change your behavior, you can change your life!"

In chapter 5, we discuss how we work with students who struggle with the most challenging behaviors. We introduce the star chart—a simple and highly effective strategy for increasing connection with these students. You will learn how to manage star charts in your classroom to remain positive, provide targeted support, and build a relationship with students who demonstrate the most challenging behaviors.

Try This!

As early as tomorrow, try using the Magic, Fuzzy Numbers strategy in your classroom. When asking students to do something, such as get out pencils or read silently, give feedback about their behavior in the form of numbers. For example:

- "Three out of four people at table four are ready."
- "Twenty-five percent of the class has their pencils ready to go. Great work. Now, 60 percent do. Awesome. I'm waiting. Now, 95 percent have them. Great job being assertive and ready to work. Let's get started." Remember, never names, always numbers.

Chapter 5

Changing the Most Challenging Behaviors With the Star Chart

> *When I put a student on a star chart, I am putting myself on one as well. It forces my focus toward positive behaviors, and it helps me redirect or ignore some less desirable ones. It can be difficult to give a reward when there are negative or disruptive things still happening, but the result of increased connection is well worth it!*
>
> **J. Gearty**, teacher, grades 7–9 ELA, personal communication, December 16, 2023

A *star chart* is a behavior modification tool commonly used to reward students for a targeted behavior. Sometimes, the star chart is publicly displayed on a student's desk, and the teacher can quickly acknowledge the desired behavior by putting a sticker or a signature on a star, as shown in figure 5.1 (page 96). Once a student earns all ten stars, then they can earn a predetermined award.

FIGURE 5.1: Example star chart for a student's desk.

When we entered the teaching profession, the star chart was a common type of award system in the classroom. Over time, they have faded in use due to their visibility when posted publicly (for example, on a student's desk or a bulletin board). We adapted this idea to create the star chart discussed in this chapter.

As teachers, most of us are open to learning new approaches to working with behavior, but in the back of our minds, we wonder how we can handle the most challenging students. We may feel like nothing will work because of how hard we have already tried to change things. Sometimes, we can even get attached to strategies not working, as this can prove we tried our hardest: "See, still nothing works." We felt the same way until the star chart came into our lives.

In this chapter, we share the story that inspired this transformative tool. Then, we break it down into all the components of how it works. What does the star chart look like? How does it work? Who can benefit from it? What good does it do?

We share how the star chart changed how we deal with the most challenging student behavior.

Not Your Average Star Chart Story

One day, our school's child psychologist, Mr. Mendive, came and quietly sat in a chair and joined our lesson. We had no idea why he was there. After forty-five minutes, he left as unobtrusively as he arrived. At the end of the day, he returned to let us know he was there to observe how we treated one of our students, Jake. Earlier that day, Jake's mom called to say that Jake hated our class, and he knew we did not like him. We were beside ourselves; this student was so challenging, and we tried to be kind and supportive, even when he was difficult. Jake was bright and in our gifted and talented program. Before he was adopted, he was also diagnosed with fetal alcohol syndrome and drug exposure in utero. His kinetic energy was a lot to handle.

So, there we were with Mr. Mendive as he went over his notes on how we treated Jake during our lesson. He pointed out that there were lots of directives, such as, "Jake, can you please stop spinning on the floor?" "Jake, can you please find a pencil?" and "Jake, can you please return to your seat?" Mr. Mendive admitted that, indeed, Jake was a handful, but that was completely beside the point; we needed to do something different. He recommended we should start by moving him from his isolated desk back into a table group. This is the *very* moment when, as a teacher, you want to start defending your actions. But instead, we said with straight faces, "OK, what can we do?"

Mr. Mendive went on to tell us that Jake only hears negative comments in our classroom. We tried to interject that we always said *please* and *thank you*, and we always tried to smile when delivering our requests to Jake. "It doesn't matter," he said. "These are *all* negative redirections." It only took a moment or two of reflection to know he was right. We know that students can quickly sense teachers' insincerity or frustration, even when the words are packaged in fancy wrapping. Because Jake was so often off task and needed redirection, we had become laser-focused on his behavior and forgot to see Jake as anything more.

Mr. Mendive's plan was for us to put Jake on a star chart and *only* say positive things to him. He said that we may need to dig deep, such as, "It's so awesome that you put on your shoes today, Jake." Star! "Thank you, Jake, for smiling at Juan at the door." Star! "I am so glad you came today." Star! Just like that. All day. Only positives. We asked, "Do you mean we cannot tell him to stop spinning on the floor?" He said, "Yes, that is exactly what I mean." That was the birth of the star chart.

Looking back, it's hard to believe we ever survived classroom teaching without the star chart. Because now, it is such a dear friend! Figure 5.2 (page 98) shows an example of a star chart we used in our classroom. It's just a few columns of stars with names at the top.

During recess, sometimes we would take a quick walk and eventually began to have a daily conversation about which student was the most challenging that day (or week). *Challenging* was the code word for a student's behavior that was making us stressed, angry, or frustrated. It could also mean we were starting to feel that the behavior was intentionally designed by the student to stop our instruction or stop other students from learning.

Admittedly, we didn't know what to do because these behaviors made our lives so hard. There is a moment as a teacher when you must get real. Sometimes, the

FIGURE 5.2: Example star chart for the classroom.

behaviors became so severe and problematic that we found ourselves feeling consistently frustrated with certain students. As adults, we'd like to avoid admitting we feel this way because it seems like we should be above this kind of thing. Jake knew how we felt; he could feel it and went home and told his mom about it. Mr. Mendive gave us the chance to do something different for Jake. Deep down, although our pride was hurt, we agreed it was important to follow through with his suggestions.

Five years later, while we were giving a tour to fifth and sixth graders around the high school, we saw Jake working on cars in the auto shop. He saw us, and he said to a friend, "That's Ms. B and Ms. Moyer. They were the best teachers!" That still chokes us up because it was so close to ending very differently.

How to Use the Star Chart

At the beginning of the school year, teachers often try to figure out where initial behavior challenges might be. After a few days, we may have a pretty good idea. From these initial observations, we try to get on top of the difficult behaviors quickly. Within the first two weeks, we meet with many of these students privately to have an honest conversation about what is going on.

We talk about their behavior and often start the conversation in front of the Tools Not Rules posters this way: "Hi, Kam, you know how I mentioned that I love honesty more than anything? I've noticed when we have time in class to work, you are often doing other things. Can you tell me about that? When did school start getting hard? When did you start getting in trouble in class? Has it happened before, or did it start in my class? You might have heard some negative things from other teachers and me. Are you okay if we *only* notice positive things? How about a star chart? After ten stars, you get a prize! What do you think?" After twenty years, and about three thousand students later, there was only one student who turned us down initially. But in no time, they tried it!

In the beginning, we want students to have a positive experience, so we might flood them with stars, whispering in their direction, "You just got another one. Only two more to go!" These students often respond with a discreet, knowing nod and a smile.

And, of course, you can start a star chart any time of the year, even during the last week of school. When you see a need or start feeling like you might be giving a student negative feedback, it's time to try one. Still, to this day, whenever we feel the "Uh-oh, I am starting to feel challenged by this student," we know we need to put them on a star chart. The star chart works wonders for both students and teachers. When you focus on the positives you see in students, you find more and more to like about them. We end up loving these students as their behaviors change.

As mentioned previously, students react positively to the focused attention of our version of the star chart. It creates a continuing dialogue between the teacher and the student about their progress and effort in the classroom. It also helps students feel seen, which helps create a positive student-teacher relationship. Some students enjoy working toward a reward for their star chart. Next, we focus on setting up rewards, maintaining privacy, and exploring the overall benefits of using a star chart in the classroom.

Rewards

At different ages or with different teachers, students learn different things. When we taught fifth and sixth grades together, students would earn a luncheon with the teacher and a friend after they earned ten stars. During lunch, we sat in a circle and shared what we noticed about the star chart student's growth. In one luncheon, we had more than ten students participating. Students would say things like, "I have noticed Tomas isn't getting as angry as much. He seems a lot happier during math." Having a peer reflect this way was so powerful. It allowed Tomas to see that his self-regulation was not only supporting his academic achievement; it was also creating social connections. Another thing that happened was that the friends of students with star charts would ask if they could be on a star chart for a behavior they wanted to change as well. We were delighted to help them, and this promoted the idea in our classroom that star charts were for everyone.

In middle school, students often tell a teacher what they want to earn when they complete their star chart. Ms. Cardoza said her eighth-grade student, Marcus, shared that he loved Hot Cheetos. So, she bought a bag to have on hand once he achieved his goal. She said it was the best $3.00 she had ever spent. Also, each year, Mr. Harris writes a small grant for prizes such as magnetic bookmarks, calculators, or earbuds. Another teacher, Ms. Jessica, has a bunch of squishy fidget balls on hand to pass out to students who earn their ten stars.

After a student fills a row of stars, we often ask, "Shall we start another row?" Sometimes, the student says, "No, I think I've got this now." This is great to see, as they have learned the lesson they needed from the chart. We can celebrate! Other times, they might say, "Yes, I'd like to do it again." Everyone knows how good it feels to hear positive things. And for some of these students, it's almost an anomaly.

Privacy

If another student notices a star chart activity and asks what it is for, we are honest. For example, "Jacque, have you ever noticed that sometimes your classmates have a hard time in class? This is one way we support them and acknowledge the good things we see them doing." Jacque shakes her head, saying, "Yeah, I know. I get it." Remember, students are deeply aware of what is going on socially, emotionally, and academically in the classroom. When we explain the star chart this way, students who are curious about it understand. We don't feel the need to point out behaviors about specific students. Instead, we reinforce that we are making an effort to help all students in the class.

If it seems like a student is struggling with the fairness of being excluded from the star chart, we offer to add their name to the chart as well. We can put them on if they wish, but 99 percent of the time, the student is happy just to understand what is happening, and they support the intent of the action.

As noted in chapter 2 (page 35), students look for adults to help them when they are struggling. They want to know you are going to try your best to help because it makes them feel safe.

Benefits

Engaging with the star chart has many benefits, even when you are dealing with the most difficult and challenging behaviors.

- **Teachers often struggle with students' difficult behaviors:** Our colleague, Mr. Gomez, admitted that his student, Korey, was ruining the entire year for him. He dreaded each day, as he knew he had to engage with her challenging behaviors every day during fifth-period science. On some days, this one student out of 130 made him feel like he didn't want to show up at work. Most teachers can relate to this, and it feels untenable.

    Using a star chart helps teachers focus on the positive instead of frustration. It allows the entire class to exhale because the focus is positive instead of a continual loop of negative redirections. Teachers enjoy their jobs more. They feel happier coming to work—and in a difficult profession, that is invaluable. Teachers are worthy of experiencing joy and happiness in their jobs, as is everyone.

- **Students with challenging and difficult behaviors often don't start struggling in your class:** These are often the students that teachers talk about together and get passed off to the next year's set of teachers with condolences. Needless to say, these students have possibly had years of negative interactions to wade through. Even as kindergarteners, they may come with a well-established history of not fitting into the norm. They start hardening off parts of themselves, and they wear these calluses like armor.

- **Students with difficult behaviors are surprised by the star chart approach, and it catches them off guard:** They are shocked to hear that you are only going to notice the good things about them. This is a great start because they are open to something different. Over time, you will notice a gentle shift in the way students show up in your class. If you have some negative interactions, you know you can go right back to the star chart to help you get back on course. Students feel this and start believing that you are going to remain connected and continue to notice good things about them, even as they work on their behavior.

Sometimes, you might wonder if it is worth it. You might doubt that positive efforts will change anything for students in the long term, so why bother? Why not just give in to what is inevitable? As mentioned previously, teacher sanity is saved, and their job satisfaction and enjoyment increase. We hypothesize that students will never forget this experience—that even for a short time, a teacher saw the good in them. That changes the story they tell themselves about who they are and who they may become someday.

- **The atmosphere in classrooms with unaddressed behaviors can be tense or ambivalent:** In classrooms with unaddressed behaviors or the general technique used for punishment is disconnection or punitive measures, the atmosphere is tense, uncomfortable, and unpredictable. Like all human beings, students value warmth and acceptance, and in classrooms like these, the warmth of support can be missing.

  Classrooms that use star charts to improve the most difficult behaviors are noticeably different. Teachers engage from a positive stance because they know how to work with and overcome the most difficult behaviors. Students feel a sense of calm and support.

On regular surveys teachers give out to assess their teaching, students often remark that their teachers support everyone. For example, in Ms. Jones's sixth-grade mathematics class, a student noted, "Ms. Jones wants everyone to learn, and she will help everyone be successful." Students make this type of comment over and over in a variety of forms. This is noteworthy because students are emphasizing the contrast to other classrooms where there may be favorites and others are ignored or targeted. They celebrate this distinction.

By using star charts, you are not rewarding bad behavior; you are trying to *change* behavior. This is an important distinction. When students are entrenched in their negative identities, it is difficult to get them to change, and they can be committed to continue reprising the same role they have played for much of their lives in school. That is possibly the hardest thing for you to do as a teacher—to see poor behavior and then follow it up by seeing something positive. There are moments when you might feel like you want to jump out of your skin like you are going against your instincts.

However, once you retrain this instinct, students trust that they will not only hear corrections but also hear positive things that create connections. This does not mean you don't immediately and emphatically address behaviors that are causing major issues for learning, but when you do, note to yourself, "Oh, Lisseth is on a star chart. I need to start noticing the good in her again." Return again and again to retraining yourself and your students to change behaviors and experiences.

Support and Reinforcements

Working with star charts does not mean you won't need additional support. There are times when we call campus security to walk a student around the halls for five minutes. In severe cases, we set up an agreement with parents so we can call home in the middle of class. We call the parents beforehand and say something like: "I love John and his sense of humor. He is very funny, and the other students love him. However, there are times when I struggle to teach because his behaviors are getting in the way. I am wondering if you could help me with this. Would it be OK if I have John call when I am struggling to teach?" Nearly every time, the parents say *yes* to this arrangement.

Genuinely asking for parents' help can be a novel experience, and often they readily agree. This also helps position parents as active participants in their child's school life. When a parent has a child who exhibits challenging behaviors, the phone calls and follow-ups from the teacher are an invitation to inspire change and follow through.

So, the next time the student is making it difficult to teach, we will call and say, for example, "Hi, I am trying to teach right now, and John keeps burping out loud to keep everyone laughing. Would you please talk to him and help him refocus?" Because we set this up beforehand with the family, the parent is happy to speak to their child to help us so we can teach. If you have a parent or guardian who is defensive about this approach, we recommend respecting their wishes. We never want to put students in an uncomfortable situation, and when parents and teachers are at a crossroads, this has a negative impact on the student. We suggest developing another plan with the student—perhaps a plan with school support staff might work just as well.

This is not shaming or "tattling." We are taking assertive action while showing love and care. We often say to students, "We love you, and your parents love you. We love you enough not to let you act this way." This type of engagement, coupled with a star chart, can be just what's needed to change students' behaviors. Students realize you are serious. They realize that *their behavior* is causing the problem, not *who they intrinsically are* as a human being. They realize that right after the phone call, we remain connected with them. We might say, "Great job handling that phone call and talking with your mom. That was really assertive. Thank you." We do not hold on to frustration or resentment. Sometimes, we just need to call in reinforcements.

Many teachers have seen a positive outcome when engaging parents in a "reverse suspension," in which a family member attends school with their child for the day. This type of situation acknowledges that we are all in this together. For those of us who are parents and have felt the challenge of this situation, we realize that parents need love and support as well. It is a good practice to set aside judgment and approach parents with the belief that all families deeply love their children. A shame-filled lecture that demeans their child or their parenting creates more disenfranchisement from school.

Simple But Effective

The concept of Occam's razor seems to be appropriate in the case of the star chart. The roots of this idea stem from the fourteenth-century logician and Franciscan friar, William of Ockham. In a nutshell, *Occam's razor* has come to mean that even with multiple solutions, the simplest one may be the best one (Gibbs, 1996). We know that the star chart may seem like a ridiculously oversimplified strategy for managing and changing challenging behaviors. We might complain about systems that are failing people and society, the lack of good values, and the absence of morals in our students. We may bemoan the current state of things and feel traumatized by factors that are, truthfully, outside of our control in the classroom.

But what we have found after two decades of working with the star chart is that it *is* that simple. It is a novel experience for a student to be noticed positively when they have become so used to the negative. It has shifted our opinion of the "challenging" student so dramatically that by the end of the year, they have become some of our favorites. It doesn't mean that it won't take tremendous effort in some cases, but if you follow through with fidelity—not perfection, but fidelity—you can make it work. Here, Occam's razor wins out.

Since 2003, countless students have benefited from the star chart. It shifts the relationship between the student and the teacher, and the hope of trust emerges and begins to flourish. We begin to see and learn amazing things about the students we never would have known. Because we are creating connections, the star chart significantly decreases the need to send students to the office for administrative intervention. It forced us to find the good in students even when they stopped believing a teacher ever would. When using a star chart, be tenaciously optimistic and persevere—it is well worth the effort!

Conclusion

In this chapter, we explored the ins and outs of using the star chart. We homed in on why it's significant to focus only on the positives. This does not mean ignoring difficult behaviors; instead, it means that in addition to receiving consequences, the student is also learning that you see the good in them, the positives. Star charts allow us to create a different communication path with students with the most challenging behaviors, and when coupled with implementing the Tools Not Rules approach in the classroom, it can be very powerful.

We also looked at the many ways this type of positive focus impacts an entire classroom—teachers, students, and families. It has been transformative for us and our students, and we believe it can be for you, too!

In the next chapter, we share all the possibilities for change that Tools Not Rules has created in schools and classrooms. Additionally, we discuss some specific challenges and difficulties we have faced and possible solutions.

Try This!

Choose a student in your class to put on a star chart. We recommend starting with one student so you can see how it goes. Choose a student who is causing you a lot of frustration and who you consider challenging due to difficult behaviors, seeking attention, apathy, or something else. Meet with the student privately and share that you would like to notice the many good things about them. Give them a couple of stars just for having a conversation with you. Remember, you are not rewarding certain behavior that you want to change. For now, you are just noticing good things about this student.

The student will be surprised by this proposition. "Do you mean I can be myself and that is good enough?" Notice the small changes in the student and yourself throughout the process. Ask yourself, "Has the student shifted their behavior in my class, even in small ways? Have I shifted my relationship with the student? Do I still see this student as challenging? What have I learned?"

Chapter 6

Overcoming Implementation Challenges and Realizing Possibilities

> *To other teachers: If you can just take the risk, it is worth it. You stop focusing on the negativity and focus on what you want to accomplish instead of worrying about what a student is going to do. I am not afraid of what they are going to do. Whatever happens, I will address it. After using Tools Not Rules, I know students are not their behaviors, and I know how to talk about and understand their behaviors.*
>
> **—J. Molesworth**, first-grade teacher, personal communication, November 19, 2023

As with all things that are created and implemented in educational spaces, a constant reflection cycle is warranted. Teachers do this daily as they plan lessons, teach lessons, and reflect on what went well and what didn't. In this chapter, we share the potential challenges and possibilities of using Tools Not Rules in the classroom. We also discuss the value of having your students fill out a Student Perception

Survey to support you in learning about how students perceive your teaching and finding out more about individual student needs.

Challenges

As teachers, we know that learning and implementing a new approach to working with students can be tough. Especially for seasoned teachers, changing what we do can feel disorienting and time-consuming (time we often don't have). In the following sections, we share some of the challenges that have emerged when teachers and administrators implement Tools Not Rules.

Getting Started With Tools Not Rules Language

One of the unique aspects of Tools Not Rules is that it establishes three language triads to help teachers and administrators coach students to become serious, assertive, and working in the classroom. To establish the foundation for Tools Not Rules, educators need to teach students the words and consciously use the language while teaching and interacting in the classroom. Sometimes, this feels a bit awkward and cumbersome until it becomes part of your routine.

When you first start the Tools Not Rules approach, it can be a little intimidating to begin using a whole new language structure and strategies (whole-class and individual adjustments and praise) that are unfamiliar. At times, you might not be sure *how* to use the language while working with students. For Tools Not Rules to have the greatest impact in the classroom, educators should spend time helping students understand the three triads and their connection to self-regulation and academic achievement.

Teachers from our Tools Not Rules study (see the appendix, page 131) shared that without having taught students what the words mean, having them act it out, or self-reflect using the words, it was difficult for them to self-assess and self-regulate with the language triads. One teacher asked students to define what the words looked like outside the classroom and in their personal lives. For example, "What does being assertive look like on the baseball field? At home? When learning to play a musical instrument? When explaining your side of a story?" This seemed to help the students connect the behaviors to the words.

Making Tools Not Rules Words Fit Every Classroom

Depending on the students you work with, some of the words in the triads might need adjustment. Older or younger students may respond to different words that

Overcoming Implementation Challenges and Realizing Possibilities 109

similarly describe the orange, green, and blue zones for working. Students who are learning English as a second language may not understand the nuances and implied meanings of the words. One teacher in our study taught English learners and found that some of the words, like *shirking*, did not translate well for her students. This teacher made the effort to translate clearly what this meant and even developed her own posters with verbal and visual cues. Similarly, when working with kindergarteners, we learned that having visuals or pictures of what each word means helped students understand the meaning, as shown in figure 6.1. (Go to www.toolsnotrules.com to purchase a set of posters for elementary students.)

Source: © 2022 by Claudia Bertolone-Smith and Marlene Moyer. Used with permission.

FIGURE 6.1: Tools Not Rules poster with pictures to help kindergartners understand the meaning of the words.

We heard from a middle school teacher who was struggling to make the words *shirking* or *showboating* work with older students. Instead, they relied on *serious* and *working* more often, as they were more effective for communicating with older students. Older students (high school) often shy away from self-identifying as *shirking* or *showboating*, and respond better to coaching toward the green zone, or *serious*, *assertive*, and *working*. For example, one teacher used Tools Not Rules language to praise a ninth-grade student: "I've noticed that you are answering questions and paying attention. I'm complimenting you because you are figuring out that you are a really great English student. I see you being serious; I see you working." (J. Gearty, personal communication, November 27, 2023).

Another teacher reflected on how older students used showboating to get attention, and they liked it, which made it hard for them to self-regulate showboating. As students get older, they do not necessarily experience the negative impacts of showboating because they become socially oriented. They tend to think it is a great way to make others laugh, and this is perceived as fun. And for older students, showing off can sometimes become mean. So, she included *showing off* in her definition of aggressive behavior. This seemed to better match what was happening in her classroom.

A fourth-grade teacher shared that she was working on coming up with clear definitions of what *showboating*, *shirking*, and *aggressive* looked and sounded like in her classroom. She posted the definitions next to her Tools Not Rules posters as follows.

- **Showboating**: Doing something for attention at the wrong time, like pretending to throw baseballs to everyone from the center of the room and saying things like, "This is sooooo boring."
- **Shirking:** Not working or taking a long time to get started or join the class.
- **Aggressive:** Being rude or impatient, using a snarky tone of voice, or incorrectly blaming others.

She focused on "using the language as frequently as possible and naming how students are embodying those descriptors because it helps them become more empowered" (A. Park, personal communication, September 27, 2023).

Another adjustment this teacher shared is that in some classes, she didn't let students act out *showboating* or *aggressive* because it became a class competition to see who could outperform each other. Therefore, the behaviors were exaggerated (like pretending to throw baseballs to friends from the center of the class as *showboating* or being loud and argumentative as *aggressive*). She found that this left out the quiet ways of showboating or being aggressive (for example, students claiming they were bored because something was too easy, taking over group work, or using an angry tone of voice). Because of the over-acting competition, students missed the opportunity to connect the words to the actions that happened in the classroom, and the true meaning of the words was construed.

The language triads we propose for Tools Not Rules provide a framework for addressing student behaviors with self-assessment and self-regulation in mind. But the same words don't always work for every class. For teachers across grade levels to truly make TNR their own, they may have to adjust the words, so they work for their particular students or classes.

Setting Parameters for Individual Student Conversations

One Tools Not Rules approach is the quick, individual conversation with a student to understand what is going on and help them self-assess and choose another approach. Sometimes, this can be a difficult process. We may need to adjust this process, such as deciding if a student has the aptitude at the moment to participate and reflect or choose to shut down the conversation (or draw the line) if there is no mutual respect.

It is important to be aware that students impacted by adverse childhood experiences (ACEs) and trauma are primed to interpret situations physiologically and demonstrate a state of fear or fight for survival. These students may identify a calm conversation as threatening and respond in flight, fight, or refusal to respond (Romero et al., 2018). Often, students who are significantly impacted by trauma may need time to calm themselves and their physiological reactions before being able to make different behavior choices.

Moreover, there are times when a student is not able to respond seriously, honestly, or respectfully to the conversation, making it highly ineffective and triggering for the teacher. We would like to highlight one teacher's story about using Tools Not Rules and *drawing the line*. This middle and high school teacher works with a challenging population of students who are impacted by rural isolation, low socioeconomic status, and one class per grade level K–12. By the time this teacher gets the students in high school, they have often been in the same class with the same people since kindergarten. It is difficult for new students to fit in and even more difficult to change behaviors and interactions that have been happening among students for years.

When this teacher engages in individual conversations about behaviors with students, she asks, "What is happening here?" She has the TNR posters available for students to reference and says that she often has them focus on the colors as well as the words. She shared that she enters the conversation with set conditions. Her "line" is that if students are cruel, mean, or disrespectful to her during the conversation, she ends it and moves to her school's discipline policy. Additionally, if the student becomes aggressive, the conversation stops (J. Howe, personal communication, November 19, 2023).

This is a model for self-regulation by setting a personal boundary and asserting that you will not accept this treatment as a human being. This is important because, as teachers, we share our humanity with students when we have conversations with them about behavior. Shawn Ginwright, author of *The Four Pivots: Reimagining Justice, Reimagining Ourselves* (2022), writes that teachers share their "curiosity, care, vulnerability, and offer human connection" (p. 115). Ginwright calls this a transformative approach to a student relationship. When using Tools Not Rules, we enter conversations with students to help them transform their behavior so they can transform their lives.

However, we should not do this work by abandoning ourselves in the process. Ginwright (2022) proposes several techniques for transformative relationships, including creating protective boundaries while living authentically, truthfully, and with a whole heart. This especially applies to teachers while using Tools Not Rules. As with any new approach, finding the right balance for individual conversations with students is part of the process.

An administrator shared that when students are sent to his office for discipline, the first thing he does is ask them for honesty and then allow them to tell their story. As human beings, having our stories heard is important, even if there are consequences for the behaviors we choose. The resulting connection and opportunity to accept the consequences with dignity are all a part of growing.

Along with the challenges of using Tools Not Rules comes a whole realm of amazing possibilities—the topic of the next section.

Possibilities

Tools Not Rules can provide a missing piece to classroom management and create a real and relevant connection with students. While we have shared many of the potential classroom benefits of using TNR throughout the book, we'd like to share a few more we learned from talking with teachers who use this approach on a daily basis.

Reducing Teacher Stress

As we developed Tools Not Rules while co-teaching fifth and sixth grades, we came to a point of calm regarding student behaviors. We accepted that students have emotions, reactions, and behaviors in the classroom. Because of Tools Not Rules, we no longer fretted about what to do about the behaviors because we had a consistent and effective plan. This, in turn, significantly lowered our stress and anxiety about addressing student behavior. We became assertive, working, serious, and happy as educators!

Overcoming Implementation Challenges and Realizing Possibilities

When we asked a first-grade teacher if Tools Not Rules reduced the stress she experienced, she was emphatic:

> Oh my goodness, yes. Using Tools Not Rules removes so many behavior issues from my classroom. Other educators can't figure out what is different. For example, I had a student teacher coming in. She kept saying, "I love the feeling of your classroom. It is peaceful." I don't have to micromanage my classroom. We are a functioning, working classroom. If I didn't have TNR, the students wouldn't understand what they were doing wrong and how to improve. It allows my first graders to be self-reflective and less embarrassed when I speak to them about their behavior choices. I tell my students I love you always; I just don't love the behavior. (J. Molesworth, personal communication, August 20, 2024)

A middle school teacher shared that Tools Not Rules "helps me, as a teacher, to stay assertive and not aggressive. Sometimes when I get frustrated, I look at the posters and think that these are the most important words in the room" (J. Gearty, personal communication, November 28, 2023). This teacher also shared that when she finds herself feeling angry or frustrated in class, she knows that it is time to use Tools Not Rules.

Another teacher shared that:

> Tools Not Rules perks up students' ears! It draws their attention back to the learning. It is an engagement and a classroom management tool. In my ten years of middle school teaching, I've read a lot of books about classroom management and classroom behavior systems. It has always been difficult to create a class that works. When I use this, I don't have as many behavior issues. They aren't as stressful for me or the others in the class. It doesn't feel good when classrooms are run with a lot of yelling. It gives students tools instead of just punishments. (M. Rios, personal communication, October 27, 2023)

Another way of looking at the possibilities of Tools Not Rules is the transformational community it can inspire. A teacher described it this way:

> It has brought a sense of community, a sense of trust, the ability to be open. It gives students the sense that 'they can,' that they can achieve academically and be a better person. Tools Not Rules offers that as a possibility. (R. Reading, personal communication, October 27, 2023)

This aligns with how Tools Not Rules alleviates stress, as your classroom foundation is built on being honest, approaching things with a seriousness of purpose, learning what it feels like to work hard and accomplish goals, and standing up for yourself by being assertive.

Increasing Student Well-Being

Many schools have adopted programs that teach students the principles of managing their emotions so they can be successful and happy in the classroom environment. We spoke with a teacher in a school who has adopted one such program. She shared that the program teaches the principles of self-assessment and self-regulation, and using Tools Not Rules gives students a chance to apply these competencies in real time and in real situations. She explained that Tools Not Rules helps students learn how to settle themselves into the green zone and take on challenges, receive and process information, and participate in learning activities (A. Park, personal communication, September 13, 2023). The real-time feedback on steps toward academic success, which is important for students who experience trauma, is an important part of this approach.

Establishing Classroom Routines and Norms

Many teachers shake students' hands and greet them as they enter the classroom to establish personal contact with each student. This can also serve as a daily check-in—who is energized, who forgot something for the school day, or who might need to check in with the school counselor before engaging in class. We loved this daily check in with our students.

For us, part of the routine was teaching students about the classroom norm for a handshake, which is also seen as a polite greeting in many parts of the United States. We taught them to stand perpendicular to the person receiving the handshake and look at them, provide a strong but not bone-crushing grip, and deliver a greeting, "Good morning!" We did this every morning with students. One student later shared with us that he got his first job, and the employer mentioned that he had a great handshake! Additionally, Marlene shared that she saw a former sixth-grade student who was now working at a local fast-food restaurant. When she saw Marlene, she walked around the counter and gave her the same firm handshake Marlene gave her at the classroom door each morning. She showed Marlene that she learned something about being assertive, and it paid off. Claudia also experienced this when seeing a former student who was now a lifeguard at the local swimming pool. The young man stopped, faced her directly, and said, "Good morning, Ms. B!" (even though it was the afternoon).

Since 2022, we have been meeting with a group of new and veteran teachers at a middle school each month to work on the application of Tools Not Rules and addressing struggles that they experience in their classrooms. We inevitably found ourselves discussing the importance of routines and how this establishes classroom norms. Routines provide the framework for the culture an educator wants to build with their class. As with everything we teach, we have to reteach, reinforce, and affirm student progress. In our conversations with teachers, we realized that Tools Not Rules can be used to do this.

In many of the conversations with students we have shared in this book, there is a common theme about helping students redirect themselves, so they are following classroom norms or school rules and policies. We also shared information from the book *Building Resilience in Students Impacted by Adverse Childhood Experiences* by Victoria Romero, Richard Robertson, and Amber Warner (2018). The book includes a wonderful list of practices that are trauma-informed, meaning an educator makes these choices because they are aware of how trauma impacts the lives of many children today. We also recognized how Tools Not Rules naturally incorporates several items on this list:

- Use clear, consistent expectations and routines.
- Teach and reteach behaviors until they become automatic.
- Solicit and incorporate student feedback.
- Be authentic and selectively vulnerable.
- Greet students at the door.
- Be a coach! Avoid power struggles by coaching students through struggles.
- Contact parents to share positive news.
- Listen without judgment.
- Maintain a calm, assertive, and respectful demeanor.

(Romero et al., 2018, pp. 90–91)

Within our group, we reflected on the need to remember the importance of well-established routines while keeping these approaches at the forefront of our teaching, no matter what our level of experience.

Another way Tools Not Rules establishes norms shared by administrators. Several noticed that when teachers are using the language in their classrooms, the language emerges as a norm for communicating about students. For example, during parent conferences, teachers discussed challenging behaviors students might show as silly, passive, or shirking. Parents and caregivers often saw similar behaviors at home and were willing to work on helping their child be more serious or assertive. Teachers also used the language to inform parents when their child was serious and working hard in the classroom or how they had become assertive by asking questions in class, which increased their understanding and performance.

A primary-grade teacher said that she reviews the language with families during Back to School Night. Then, when she needs to call home, the parents understand what she is trying to communicate because they know the meaning and intent of the Tools Not Rules language. For example, when she might call to share that "Ben is working hard on not shirking and not being silly but could use some more support from home." Parents understand the behaviors that are getting in the way of Ben's learning. She says parents are grateful for understanding the Tools Not Rules language and suggests they use it with their children at home (J. Molesworth, personal communication, August 20, 2024). Parents and caregivers can praise their children for being hardworking and serious about school, which increases the development of a growth mindset (Dweck, 2016).

The Tools Not Rules language also started to appear in emails to parents, individualized education plans (IEPs), and weekly student updates. There is a unique possibility for growth and understanding when teachers, parents, and students share common knowledge of words used at school. This also establishes a norm for how educational professionals discuss student behavior.

Student Perception Survey

As educators, we know that there are a tremendous number of events, responses, and actions that happen during the school day. It is possible that we may miss some things or not have enough information to interpret student behaviors, engagement, or motivation accurately. Sometimes, we have shy students who don't say much, and

Overcoming Implementation Challenges and Realizing Possibilities 117

their behavior flies below our radar. We might not be sure about their experiences learning with us or what they might need because their behaviors are not emergencies.

To find out more about possible unseen undercurrents occurring in the classroom, we use a Student Perception Survey. This survey asks students about inclusion, community, connection, and perceptions of the teacher. Similar to the school climate survey featured in the appendix (see figure A.1, page 136), it uses a Likert scale from 1–5 (1–Never, 2–Rarely, 3–Sometimes, 4–Often, and 5–Always or most always) as well as short-answer questions. Figure 6.2 shows an example of the student perception survey we used in our middle school classroom.

For each item, circle the number that best describes how you feel about the statement.

I feel included in our classroom community.

1	2	3	4	5
Never	Rarely	Sometimes	Often	Always or most always

I feel safe in our classroom community.

1	2	3	4	5
Never	Rarely	Sometimes	Often	Always or most always

My teacher helps me understand how to improve my work.

1	2	3	4	5
Never	Rarely	Sometimes	Often	Always or most always

I understand how this class connects to the real world.

1	2	3	4	5
Never	Rarely	Sometimes	Often	Always or most always

My teacher cares about me.

1	2	3	4	5
Never	Rarely	Sometimes	Often	Always or most always

FIGURE 6.2: Student perception survey.

continued →

> **Complete each statement. Be as detailed as possible.**
>
> One thing I appreciate about how my teacher teaches me is:
>
> It would help me if my teacher did this one thing:
>
> What else do you want to share? Include how you feel at school, things at home, anything at all!

*Visit **go.SolutionTree.com/behavior** for a free reproducible version of this figure.*

Asking students to provide feedback and information about how they feel in your class is an excellent way to make sure you are addressing the needs of all students. Modeling for students the skill of receiving and applying constructive feedback helps them understand how they might do this themselves (Romero et al., 2018). This demonstrates to students that their experiences and perceptions matter and encourages them to advocate for themselves in constructive ways.

We recommend conducting this survey twice per year for elementary students and once per trimester for middle and high school students. Before giving the survey, emphasize to students that there are no right answers and ask that they just answer as honestly as they can. You want to avoid students answering based on what they think you, the teacher, want them to say or what they think their friends expect them to say. Instead, ask them to feel their way to their answers, just like we ask them to find honesty in their heart, not their head.

In addition, you might consider revising the survey to include some content-related questions that help you gauge student understanding of and engagement in certain subjects or academic areas, such as the following.

- How does what we learn in English language arts (or your content) connect to the real world or your future?
- How well do you understand the concepts we are learning right now in mathematics?
- Tell me about our class assignments—do they challenge you in a good way?

- What is something I can do as a teacher to help you succeed in our class?

Once all students have taken the survey, review each student's answers individually. Since you can administer the survey on a Google Form, you can click through each response. This lets you sit with each student's answers for a while. It can be gratifying, as students can be generous with their positive feedback and provide indicators of things that are happening in their lives. As you read individual responses, note any students whose responses are 2 or lower on the scale. After you make your list, have a quick, quiet check-in with these students over the next week or two.

Here is a great way to start: "Hi, thanks so much for your honesty on the survey. I see you scored our classroom a 2 for feeling safe. Can you tell me more?" Or, "You circled a 1 on the statement: *My teacher cares about me*. I am so sorry to hear this. Can you tell me what makes you feel this way?" The survey can provide some surprising and often significant insights into how students are feeling and what experiences they are having both inside and outside the classroom.

There are several ways the survey results can help create a greater awareness of students' needs in the classroom. You can gain significant insights into how students are feeling or understanding a situation from a student's perspective. It can be daunting when a student gives us low scores on our performance, but we can also see this as a chance to learn more about the student and our teaching practices. Students may also share something that requires support beyond the classroom. Even a small comment might indicate a larger problem, and this provides school personnel a chance to address this need.

Obtaining Significant Insights

Conducting this survey may seem time-consuming or uncomfortable; however, it is amazing what happens in our classrooms that we do not know about. Students often feel more comfortable writing about their feelings than talking about them. For example, for the prompt, *Share something you wish your teacher would change or could do to help me more*, a student (we will call him Mason) responded, "I wish she wouldn't target me because of my skin." The teacher who had given the survey reflected on what had been happening in class and realized what this student said was true. Mason was the only African American in her class. In one lesson, she had asked him to expand on the language used in a poem by a southern Black poet. The teacher immediately knew she had put Mason on the spot, and at that moment, he could hardly get a word out of his mouth. He had no forewarning and, like most students, had not thought about the poem.

The teacher did not consciously call on Mason because he was African American, but in retrospect, she could fully understand why Mason felt this way. In this situation, Mason felt he was expected to be an expert because both he and the author are Black. The teacher was horrified when she realized her mistake and was impressed by Mason's courage in sharing this honest response. This allowed for an honest conversation, which included a heartfelt apology from the teacher. After the apology, Mason opened up more in class and shared how much he liked it. Had the teacher not given the survey, this information would most likely never come to light, and a year of connection through instruction would have been lost.

Meeting with each student takes commitment, as there may be several students who need a one-on-one conversation. What you will find is that some students might have made an error in the rating, or conversely, as with Mason, have something very important to share. Overall, getting a chance to provide feedback makes students feel seen and heard. It makes them trust that we care about their experience in our classrooms.

Finding the Meaning Behind Low Scores

Pay close attention to students who give low scores across the board. It can be hard not to take this personally and respond accordingly; however, these are the students who are the most desperate for change to occur. It is a good idea to start with these conversations first. After one particular survey, we checked in with Evie because she rated the class experience as 2s or lower across the board. When we asked her about it, she said it didn't have to do with our class but that she feels tremendous anxiety all the time at school. We were able to refer Evie to the counseling department and wellness center.

In a colleague's classroom, a student scored the classroom environment and instruction the lowest possible score across the board. Benny was on this teacher's radar, and yet she was still struggling to create a positive relationship with him. She had been avoiding putting him on a star chart (see chapter 5, page 95) because she wasn't aware of how Benny experienced her class. The survey results inspired her to put Benny on a star chart, not because he needed it, but because she needed to increase connection and build a relationship with Benny to help him feel seen and included in the classroom. This created a total turnaround in her experience with Benny and his response to her classroom.

Reviewing the overall data allows you to see what students perceive as your strengths and what you need to focus on. This might connect to relationships (students feeling connected to the classroom community) or your instruction (connecting the real world to the content). This is direct feedback from students; they will notice when you adjust to accommodate their needs, which sends a significant message that you care.

Identifying and Attending to Students' Personal Issues

You may be able to identify a variety of student issues from these surveys. Students may share personal experiences that should be passed along to the counseling department. They may share experiences of loneliness, abuse, or just funny facts that allow you to reach out and ask some questions. This gives you an opportunity to have conversations with students about what they have shared. Here is an example of how you might approach such a conversation.

One year, a middle school student, Leah, had an interesting response to the short-answer prompt, *What else do you want to share? Include how you feel at school, things at home, anything at all!* She wrote, "I am happy to be at school because I feel so lonely at home." When her teacher followed up, the student shared that her single mom is never home due to working late each night. She is often home with her older sister, who doesn't engage with her. The teacher asked what she would like to do about it and suggested possibly seeing the counselor or going to the wellness center to visit a therapist. Leah said nothing needed to be done at the moment, but she just wanted to share this with her teacher. The teacher knew that Leah needed to share something that was difficult for her. The teacher responded, "I see that. That sounds hard." She offered real empathy.

So often, as adults, we feel like we need to fix things or are unsure of what to do. As long as safety isn't an issue, we just need to stand in witness to students' experiences. Say, "I hear that, and that is hard." It is dignifying as a human being to hear these few words reflected. It says, "You are not alone."

In this conversation, Leah wanted her teacher to know about her feeling lonely. The teacher was present and heard her situation. The teacher also reflected, "That sounds really hard." Sometimes, when students share difficult experiences, we may feel we need to have the answer to the problem or give advice. However, it takes tremendous vulnerability and trust to share what is difficult in our lives. We can listen and affirm that the situation is difficult. We can offer support that might help and stay connected to this student by checking in. You might consider asking students who share personal issues to give you a number from 1–5 (with 1 as poor and 5 as great) each day about how things are going when you greet them at the door. This gives you the opportunity to keep a close eye on the student and watch for negative changes.

Please note that there are exceptions to the rule of "just listening" and not getting involved. If a student shares that they feel they are in danger, considering self-harm, or are being abused in any way, you need to report this immediately.

Done well, honest and shame-free conversations based on survey results are uniquely effective. Giving the Student Perception Survey can allow you to find and mend student issues occurring in your classroom. The time spent is well worth the results.

Conclusion

In this chapter, we discussed the challenges and opportunities of using Tools Not Rules in the classroom. As with any new approach to teaching, it takes time for this to feel natural within your teaching style. Some teachers choose to adjust the language to meet the needs of their students for more successful results. Teachers can also model assertiveness themselves by drawing the line if they must during individual student conversations.

We also shared some possibilities that emerged from using Tools Not Rules in classrooms and schools. From educators and administrators who have used it, we learned that it can help reduce teacher stress, increase student well-being, and help develop important classroom norms. Soliciting and responding to student feedback is an important way to establish a safe and connected classroom. One way you can do this is by giving your students the student perception survey (see figure 6.2, page 117). We discussed the importance of taking this feedback seriously and using it to check in with students who appear to be struggling to find out more. Using what we learn in these conversations to make changes to address students' needs is powerful. This allows us to show our students that we are listening and that we care.

Try This!

Create a survey for students. You can base it on the student perception survey in figure 6.2 (page 117) or create something that better meets your and your students' specific needs. After conducting the survey, review each student's response. Note any score that is 2 or lower and short answers that direct you to probe a bit further.

Remember to start follow-up conversations by showing appreciation for students' honesty, such as, "Thank you so much for your honesty. I see you scored a 2 on (item). You said (response). Can you share more about that?" These follow-up conversations should take no longer than thirty seconds. See what you find out. Your students will appreciate your interest and thoughtful, caring interactions with them.

Epilogue
Moving Forward

Teachers are masters at moving forward. We are responsible for the emotional, social, and academic progress of our students, and we are constantly planning, preparing, and implementing learning in our classrooms to ensure student success. We move students forward from one grade level to the next. And even after our most difficult day at school, we move forward to the next morning with hope and determination to make things better.

We hope using the Tools Not Rules approach allows you to take care of yourself as you educate your students. We hope that as you move forward into your next day or new year of teaching, you will find that sweet spot of constructing an honest, serious and hardworking class, where all sorts of learning magic can happen. And we hope you have some new ideas to complement the great work you already do.

At the beginning of the school year, we posted the poem "Invitation" by Shel Silverstein (1978) on our classroom door to welcome new students. This poem invites all students into the classroom, including dreamers, wishers, liars, hopers, prayers, magic-bean buyers, and pretenders. The last line beckons, if you any are one of these: "Come sit by the fire, for we have some flax-golden tales to spin. Come in! Come in!" (Silverstein, 1978, p. 9). We love this invitation to join the classroom for a year of learning and community comprised of a unique set of individuals where each becomes *communessential* (a word a former student created to describe how every single person in the class is needed to create our community). The first day of school is full of surprises—some good and some thought provoking. If you are lucky, you may get a day of dreamy student behavior before you really start to understand who is in your class. Then, the true work of a teacher begins.

If you have made it to this part of the book, our hope is that you are ready to use Tools Not Rules to work with your dreamers, wishers, liars, hopers, prayers, magic-bean buyers, and pretenders. We are fully aware of the time and energy it takes to implement something new in the classroom, and we are excited about the possibilities this opportunity offers. From here, we hope you embrace the following three concepts on your journey: (1) confidence, (2) courage, and (3) community.

Confidence in Your Ability to Handle Challenging Behaviors

Before Tools Not Rules, we both spent many evenings worrying about what happened at school, fretting about student behaviors we weren't sure how to address, or feeling frustrated and upset about an incident with a student. This meant we were not able to truly be present with our own relationships and families or would stay late at work trying to think of solutions to the situations. Each incident seemed like a new crisis. Essentially, our work-life balance was dramatically unbalanced, and we were just trying to survive.

Once we created and started using the strategies, language, and philosophy of Tools Not Rules, all this drastically changed. The fretting transformed to confidence—we regularly witnessed students assessing and regulating their behavior with the outcome of increased academic success and happiness in the classroom. That meant we didn't need to take these situations home with us as they were resolving. We began to see student reactions and behaviors as part of teaching rather than obstacles to our teaching.

The amount of energy spent worrying about how to work with showboating or shirking behavior diminished. Our confidence grew as teachers because students were making academic progress, and our classroom community was stronger than ever. Tools Not Rules provided a solid foundation to stand on, and we no longer had to critically analyze each incidence of student behavior. Our emotional reactions to the situations diminished, and we were able to close our doors at the end of the day and be present for the other important parts of our lives.

We want this for you too. If you try one thing or everything in this book, we hope it leads to a growing confidence that there is a plan in place that addresses behaviors consistently and effectively, and that this confidence leads to a satisfying sense of accomplishment and happiness in your classroom.

Courage to Create the Classroom You and Your Students Deserve

A big part of working with and teaching students is knowing and trusting yourself. For every moment you spend with students in the school environment, envision what students need to do to learn and how you will ensure it happens. For example, if you want quiet reading during ELA time, how will you make it happen? If you want students to calmly enter the classroom and get out their mathematics tools, how will you make it happen? As educators, find the courage to be assertive and serious about establishing and reinforcing what you want in the classroom, and this is no small thing. Finding the balance between empathy (showing you understand how difficult something can be) and insistence (reinforcing and managing structures and routines for learning) can be a challenge.

A student teacher who was struggling with student behavior once told us that they didn't want to "be mean" to the students by making them do what she requested. We challenged this approach by telling her that students need to know she means it when she teaches and upholds routines in class. Meaning it is not mean; instead, it increases the safety and support students feel in the classroom. Using Tools Not Rules helps educators develop and sustain boundaries. It guides them in upholding the green zone: serious, assertive, and working.

Tools Not Rules can help you find your boundaries and hold them. It helps you see students separate from their behavior and eloquently address the situation. You do not have to put up with rude behavior or apathy from students. However, you must find a way to address it productively. When you find the courage to flip the script and ask the students what is going on instead of telling them what they are or what they are not doing, you can ignite their curiosity about themselves. You can support and connect with even the most troublesome students, without giving yourself away. We wish this for you too—growing courage means you can begin to love *all* your students, hold to your boundaries, and inspire academic, social, and emotional transformation.

Community of Educators Who Support Each Other and Students in Their Ability to Change

Having a "bad day" as a teacher can be devastating, gut-wrenching, and isolating. You might feel embarrassed, ashamed, and deeply troubled. Both novice and experienced teachers have days like this. This can make you close our classroom doors, disconnect, and silently absorb this disappointment, frustration, and trauma. Or you might engage in complaining conversations that disparage the student, their family, and their situation. This might help you blow off some steam, but it can also cause you to justify disconnecting from the student.

Through our own experiences and talking with teachers who use Tools Not Rules, we have learned that we prefer to problem solve with other teachers who use this approach. This is because the conversation is less about the student and more about the behavior. It is more about finding solutions versus sitting in our own shame of not having the right strategies. Instead, we wonder about what the student is trying to communicate with the behavior and what they might need. We brainstorm ideas to help: Do we need another individual conversation? Do we need a star chart? Often, we consult with a student's favorite teacher in the school to ask how they connect and remain productive. A colleague might volunteer to meet with you and the student at recess to help with the conversation and gain deeper insight.

We have been regularly working with a group of educators each month at a middle school, and we collectively discuss student behaviors using the Tools Not Rules approach. Teachers share success ("The star chart worked!") and struggles ("My students want to taste all the white powders in our chemistry lab!"). We offer ideas and information ("I have that student in fifth period, and this really works"). We leave the meetings filled with hope and sometimes joy. We know that we are not alone, and we have others who understand and support us.

When we are vulnerable and reach out to colleagues, we eradicate the isolation that shame can cause. We feel buoyed by the camaraderie and community of people who want to help us as well as our students. We wish this community for you as you tackle the multitude of behaviors that colleagues can understand. Reach out to us if you are alone in this work. Let's find a way to connect you to others.

In Closing

One thing we haven't shared is how Tools Not Rules has had an impact on our personal behavior *outside* the classroom. We constantly use Tools Not Rules to navigate our own lives, and we wonder if we are being passive when the situation needs us to be assertive. We pull back on showboating because we recognize that it can be a destructive force. We often catch ourselves shirking (especially when needing to grade assignments) and self-regulate to make sure we allow time to get our work done. Tools Not Rules also helps us understand the motivations of others in our lives. We recognize when people are coming at us with aggression and know that this may be an overreaction to something painful. Moreover, Tools Not Rules is instrumental in helping us meet our own children's needs.

Tools Not Rules has opened our hearts and minds as educators and as human beings. We hope this work will find others who need it right now. We send this out with great respect for the educators in our lives, both past and present. We honor your teaching path, and if Tools Not Rules is part of your journey, we are incredibly grateful to be a part of it.

Appendix
The Tools Not Rules Study

In order to take a closer look at how Tools Not Rules impacts students and teachers in the classroom, we decided to set up a research study to see what evidence and data we could gather about its effectiveness. The study was conducted at a rural West Coast middle school during the 2020–2021 school year.

While planning this study the previous spring, we were suddenly stunned by the pandemic—how it entered our lives and how schoolwide instruction was severely impacted. When considering whether to move forward with the study or postpone it due to COVID-19, we were pleasantly surprised when the administration and the teaching staff overwhelmingly agreed to forge ahead. So, we did, and in this surprising and disorienting time in public education, we uncovered both interesting and astonishing things about implementing Tools Not Rules in a middle school environment. This chapter shares how we conducted the study and the results we found.

Tools Not Rules Study Background

Middle school students (grades 6–8) are at a unique time in their lives. They are balancing the need for independence from family while often codependent with peers. They strive to be

themselves while concurrently being both positively and negatively impacted by the social culture in school. Teaching middle school students offers both challenges and opportunities to build resilient, engaged, and well-adjusted individuals ready to take on more academic challenges and personal responsibility. Joy Rose and Sam Steen (2014) describe resiliency in the school environment as the "ability to bounce back from challenging circumstances."

Middle schools often use behavioral systems in hopes that they will have a positive and productive culture. Some of these systems include positive behavior intervention and support (PBIS), restorative justice, and multitiered systems of support (MTSS). Sometimes, these behavioral approaches require expensive training and upkeep, and teachers and administrators can tire of implementing elaborate systems with little positive or permanent shifts in culture or student behavior. Tools Not Rules is a simple and direct approach to working with students, yet it has the potential to create deep connections and lasting positive change.

At the very core of Tools Not Rules is the goal of helping students develop the ability to take the initiative to discover what's going on within themselves and their feelings (self-assessment) and then choose different behaviors to generate more successful outcomes (self-regulation). The Collaborative for Academic, Social, and Emotional Learning (CASEL, n.d.) created a framework that promotes the following five broad areas of social-emotional learning (SEL).

- **Self-awareness:** The ability to understand one's own emotions, thoughts, and values and how they influence behavior across contexts.

- **Self-management:** The ability to manage one's emotions, thoughts, and behaviors effectively in different situations and to achieve goals and aspirations.

- **Responsible decision-making:** The ability to make caring and constructive choices about personal behavior and social interactions across diverse situations.

- **Relationship skills:** The ability to establish and maintain healthy and supportive relationships and to navigate settings with diverse individuals and groups.

- **Social awareness:** The ability to feel compassion for others, understand broader historical and social norms for behavior in different settings, and recognize family, school, and community resources and supports.

Self-awareness and self-assessment (embedded in self-management) are critical steps in human development, especially in academic environments (CASEL, n.d.). These are the focus of Tools Not Rules.

One concern is that adolescents often use technology to avoid stress, and it appears this negatively impacts the development of self-regulation and dealing with challenging situations (Twenge, 2017). Experiencing and managing strong emotions are important skills developed in childhood and adolescence to boost internal regulatory processes, which are essential components of mental health (Hoge, Bickham, & Cantor, 2017). During our study, we wanted to investigate if Tools Not Rules impacted students' ability to honestly self-assess and take steps toward self-management through different behavior choices. Specifically, we were interested in teachers', students', and administrators' reflections on the benefits and drawbacks of Tools Not Rules over the yearlong study.

Because the middle school we worked with was using the Marzano and colleagues (2018) high reliability schools framework, the administration was interested to see if Tools Not Rules would have an impact on the first level of this framework: "Creating a safe, supportive, and collaborative culture within the school" (Marzano et al., p. 37). Tools Not Rules is a teaching approach that educators can use to create a classroom culture that is safe, supportive, and collaborative. The Marzano framework also highlights the need for school staff and faculty to develop this type of community among themselves (Marzano et al., 2018). In our study, we investigated if Tools Not Rules was an effective tool for creating this kind of learning environment.

School Demographics and Study Participants

Our middle school study site is in a rural area of a western state with striking dichotomies. Those who own homes or vacation in the area can be among the wealthiest in the United States; however, those who work in the service industry that supports tourism can often struggle with poverty and homelessness. Based on data from the National Center for Education Statistics (2022–23) for this area, 52 percent of students receive free or reduced lunch, while 2.5 percent of students living in the county experience shelter insecurity (KidsData, 2024). The school includes a diverse population with 53.7 percent minority enrollment (U.S. News, 2024). In mathematics achievement, 31 percent of students met the standard, while 69 percent scored below the standard. In English language arts, 42 percent performed at or above the standard, while 58 percent fell below the standard (U.S. News, 2024).

Because of the COVID-19 school closures, students were engaged in online learning in the fall and allowed to return to school in the spring during the period of the study. COVID-19 caused many tourism industries that employed students' parents to temporarily or permanently close. Data USA (n.d.) reports that 25.4 percent of residents in the town work for the tourism industry in the area. This may have increased the likelihood that students who hovered above the poverty or homeless level might have slid further into these situations during this year.

The staff and administration at the site were courageous by taking on this work in the middle of a worldwide pandemic. They were committed to building an increasingly safe, collaborative, and supportive culture at the school despite the turmoil. Against all odds, they wanted to work toward a solution for their students in this paradigm. Following are the elements of what we implemented at the school site during the 2020–2021 school year.

- Initially, thirty-two teachers, staff, and administrators participated in a Tools Not Rules training in the spring before we started the study. This allowed them to get a sense of the program and understand how it works in the classroom.
- In the fall, we offered a yearlong professional development course teaching how to use Tools Not Rules that met twenty times during the school year. Teachers were paid for their time and could also receive university continuing education credits. School staff and faculty were always welcome to participate in the professional development; it was a flexible opportunity.
- Attendance at these trainings varied throughout the timeframe. On average, we would have between fifteen and twenty teachers at each professional development session.
- Eleven teachers agreed to participate in the yearlong study on the impact of Tools Not Rules. These teachers agreed to attend all professional development sessions and implement Tools Not Rules in their classrooms for the year.
- The principal and both vice principals agreed to be part of the study by implementing the Tools Not Rules approach, attending the professional development when available, and participating in three group interviews throughout the year.

- Twelve middle school students agreed to participate in two online focus-group interviews about Tools Not Rules. Students were interviewed in December and June of the school year. All student volunteers had parental permission to participate.
- The administration made it possible for study participants to observe each other teaching and using Tools Not Rules for brief periods (twenty minutes) during the school day. Teacher participants were asked about this experience in their one-on-one interviews.

Data Gathering and Analysis

As mentioned in the preceding section, throughout the school year, study participants attended a yearlong professional development focused on Tools Not Rules implementation. Site administrators would join when available. The curriculum covered how to implement Tools Not Rules in the classroom, including how to teach students the language and practice using the language during whole-group instruction and one-on-one conversations. We also conducted a book study on Jensen's (2019) book, *Poor Students, Rich Teaching: Seven High-Impact Mindsets for Students From Poverty (Using Mindsets in the Classroom to Overcome Student Poverty and Adversity)* because of how his work on teacher mindsets complemented the application of Tools Not Rules in the classroom. Our study focused on the following two questions.

1. Does Tools Not Rules help create a safe, collaborative, and supportive learning environment for students?
2. Does Tools Not Rules help students develop self-assessment and self-regulation skills?

We collected data in the following ways.

- We created a school climate survey, which we administered at the beginning and the end of the school year to all teachers and administrators (see figure A.1, page 136).
- We conducted interviews with study participants (administrators, teachers, and students who agreed to participate in focus groups). We purposely chose to interview students in groups for their interview comfort. Teachers, administrators, and student focus groups were interviewed twice.

Figure A.1 shows the school climate survey we used with school staff at the beginning and end of the school year. The school climate survey uses a Likert scale of 1–5 (1–Never, 2–Rarely, 3–Sometimes, 4–Often, and 5–Always or almost always).

For each item, circle the number that best describes your school culture.

We are developing our capacity for positive connection between students and staff.

1	2	3	4	5
Never	Rarely	Sometimes	Often	Always or most always

We use effective teaching strategies.

1	2	3	4	5
Never	Rarely	Sometimes	Often	Always or most always

We give students an opportunity to self-assess and identify their feelings about what caused an issue.

1	2	3	4	5
Never	Rarely	Sometimes	Often	Always or most always

We encourage students to self-regulate by choosing different behaviors in order to increase their success.

1	2	3	4	5
Never	Rarely	Sometimes	Often	Always or most always

We collaborate about how to effectively engage students.

1	2	3	4	5
Never	Rarely	Sometimes	Often	Always or most always

We encourage and expect honest interactions with students.

1	2	3	4	5
Never	Rarely	Sometimes	Often	Always or most always

We effectively deal with student behavior, so it does not get in the way of instruction.

| ① Never | ② Rarely | ③ Sometimes | ④ Often | ⑤ Always or most always |

We feel that students are engaged and want to learn.

| ① Never | ② Rarely | ③ Sometimes | ④ Often | ⑤ Always or most always |

We support each other when we are challenged with difficult student behavior.

| ① Never | ② Rarely | ③ Sometimes | ④ Often | ⑤ Always or most always |

We feel that some students are a disruption to the learning of all students.

| ① Never | ② Rarely | ③ Sometimes | ④ Often | ⑤ Always or most always |

We feel stressed by some student behavior.

| ① Never | ② Rarely | ③ Sometimes | ④ Often | ⑤ Always or most always |

All students with behavior challenges turn in assignments on a regular basis.

| ① Never | ② Rarely | ③ Sometimes | ④ Often | ⑤ Always or most always |

We have a strong, positive connection with all students.

| ① Never | ② Rarely | ③ Sometimes | ④ Often | ⑤ Always or most always |

FIGURE A.1: School climate survey.

Visit go.SolutionTree.com/behavior to download a free reproducible version of this figure.

Table A.1 (page 138) outlines the study participants, the type of data collected and analysis, and the frequency of data collection.

TABLE A.1: Data Collection From Tools Not Rules Study

Participants	Data Collection and Type of Analysis	Frequency
School administration	Group interviews, recorded and transcribed (qualitative analysis)	Three interviews (fall, winter, and spring)
Teachers (eleven participants)	Individual interviews, recorded and transcribed (qualitative analysis)	Two interviews (winter and spring)
Student focus group (twelve student participants)	Group interview (three to six participants in each interview), recorded and transcribed (qualitative analysis)	Two focus-group interviews (winter and spring)
School climate survey (sent to entire school staff)	Likert scale data (quantitative analysis)	Beginning and end of the school year

Data Analysis Results

We analyzed the survey data by calculating the average score for each statement for the beginning-of-the-year survey (early September, number of responders [n] = 38) and the end-of-the-year survey (early June, n = 35). We then calculated the difference between the means and the percent change between beginning and ending surveys. For example, a change of 10.93 percent indicated that there was a 10.93 percent rise in agreement in the Likert scale data. A negative percentage (for example, −15.49 percent) indicates that the percentage in agreement dropped.

Table A.2 shows the survey results and percentage of growth or decline for the beginning-of-the-year (pre) and end-of-the-year (post) school culture surveys.

TABLE A.2: Pre and Post School Culture Survey Results

Question	Average Score (Pre)	Average Score (Post)	Difference	Percent Change
We are developing our capacity for positive connection between students and staff.	3.66	4.06	0.4	10.93%

TABLE A.2: Pre and Post School Culture Survey Results

Question	Average Score (Pre)	Average Score (Post)	Difference	Percent Change
We use effective teaching strategies.	3.82	3.94	0.12	3.14%
We give students an opportunity to self-assess and identify their feelings about what caused an issue.	3.08	3.63	0.55	17.8%
We encourage students to self-regulate by choosing different behaviors in order to increase their success.	3.00	3.77	0.77	25.67%
We collaborate about how to effectively engage students.	3.29	3.85	0.56	17.02%
We encourage and expect honest interactions with students.	3.74	4.09	0.35	9.36%
We effectively deal with student behavior, so it does not get in the way of instruction.	2.95	3.46	0.51	17.29%
We feel students are engaged and want to learn.	3.37	3.66	0.29	8.61%
We support each other when we are challenged with difficult student behavior.	3.97	4.03	0.06	1.51%
We feel that some students are a disruption to the learning of all students.	3.55	3.00	−0.55	−15.49%
We feel stressed by some student behavior.	3.34	2.57	−0.77	−23.05%
All students with behavior challenges turn in assignments on a regular basis.	2.32	2.46	0.14	6.03%
We have a strong, positive connection with all students.	3.71	4.03	0.32	8.63%

Additionally, we calculated the difference in percent change between teachers in the study who were implementing Tools Not Rules for the school year and teachers who chose not to. Figure A.2 shows the comparison of the percentage change between these two groups for the featured statements. We specifically chose these statements, as they are deeply connected to using Tools Not Rules in the classroom.

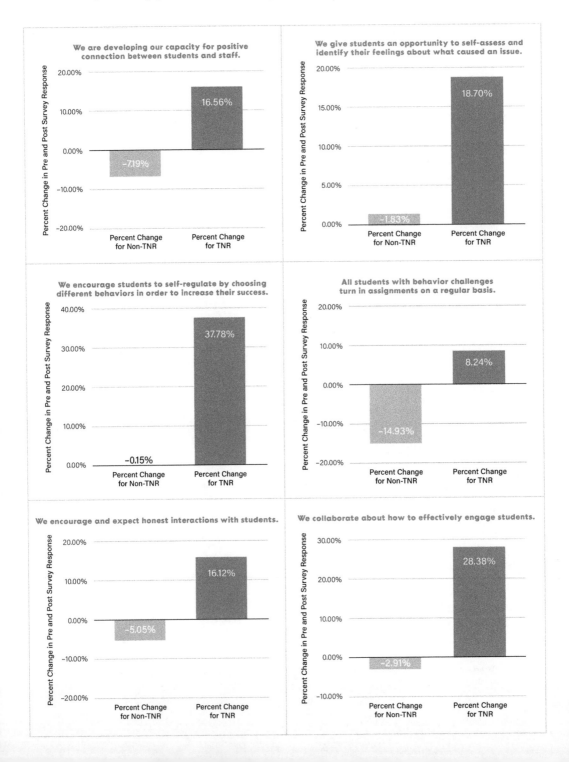

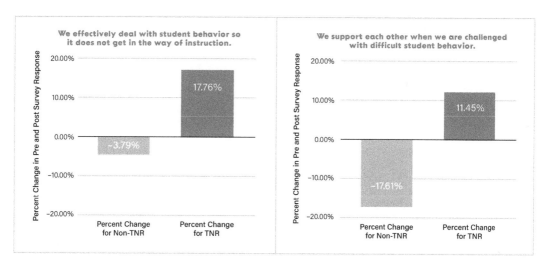

FIGURE A.2: Percent change on selected statements comparing teachers who participated in the Tools Not Rules training and those who did not.

- We looked for commonalities among what was said by participants and then grouped these into themes for each group. For example, based on student interview data, we found students often mentioned that Tools Not Rules helped them change their behavior, and they often talked about the difference between classrooms that used TNR and those that did not. Therefore, these two concepts became themes for the student interviews.
- Once we established themes from the interview transcripts, we went back and found statements that further described each theme. For example, for the theme of TNR teacher impact, we identified statements such as "Tools Not Rules transformed the way I approached being an educator" and "This language has changed everything for me because I'm not fighting them [students], and they're doing their own kind of self-reflection." One teacher stated, "If you change the way you speak with kids, it helps you be happier."
- Based on sorted statements and themes, we generated a synthesized statement from interview data that described each theme.

Tables A.3–A.5 (pages 142–145) show the overarching themes and synthesized statements from the administrator, teacher, and student focus-group interviews.

TABLE A.3: Administrator Interviews

Themes From Administrator Interviews	Synthesized Statements From Administrators
Training logistics	• Teachers need additional support on how to authentically use the language from the TNR posters. Teachers' use of TNR may depend on their comfort levels and whether they hear positive feedback from other teachers. Increasing teaching rounds (observations) has been helpful in training.
Teachers' use of TNR language with students (based on classroom observation)	• Administrators see positive interactions (more honesty, less negativity) and better relationships in classrooms using TNR. Some teachers don't think TNR language matches their personality type. There are cases in which teachers shame students while using the language, indicating a need for further reflection and training.
TNR student impact	• There is a noticeable change in student behavior in classes where teachers utilize TNR. Students behave better, express enthusiasm, and are more engaged in the classroom. Administrators witness increased engagement, students understanding the language, and positive behavioral change.
Teacher impact	• TNR appears to have made a difference in the classroom. Teachers' relationships with students are better because the language changes their approach, while possibly also changing teachers' behaviors. Using TNR appears to be tied to better classroom discipline and less discipline issues with students.
Connecting to other site initiatives (for example, Marzano high reliability schools [Marzano et al., 2018])	• There is a general consensus that TNR and Marzano programs work well together without any noted conflict.
Continuing to make TNR a priority	• TNR is making an impact at this middle school, and sharing this with a wider audience might help further implement TNR in more classrooms. It seems previous methods are not as effective as the change TNR is bringing. • Administrators can include more collaborative conversations, create a roadmap for future goals and accomplishments of TNR, and allow open participation (for example, allowing teaching to join PD and activities whenever they like).

Appendix

TABLE A.4: Participating Teacher Interviews

Themes From Teacher Interviews	Synthesized Statements From Teachers
Benefits of using TNR in my classroom	- TNR produces a positive shift in the classroom environment for teacher-student communication and relationships. Students are more open about what they need from teachers. - Teachers believe TNR has changed their teaching style and the ways they engage with students. - TNR uses words to identify student behavior, which allows teachers to label behaviors instead of students, with less generalization, more respect, and more compassion. - TNR words empower teachers and help develop a no-shame approach to working with disruptive behaviors.
What teachers are continuing to work on in order to implement TNR	- Implementing TNR seems to be difficult across languages (for example, from English to Spanish) and would benefit more students if it was properly translated into those languages. - Teachers express a general consensus that they just need to use TNR more, consistently, and readily as well as make themselves more comfortable with the language. - A few comments mention using TNR in the beginning and then falling out of it. - Teachers also mention individual things they'd like to do with TNR for their classroom. One teacher notes they want to "frame what serious, assertive, and working looks like before they begin independent practice," which implies that showing what TNR behaviors look like may result in better productivity. - Another teacher mentions wanting to weave in TNR with end-of-day classroom reflection.
Using the TNR language with students and developing comfort with words	- Students understand TNR when teachers use the language, and repetition from other teachers helps students pick up the language better. - TNR helps teachers dismiss assumptions and understand students from a more compassionate place. - Teachers report better in-the-moment self-assessment of their words and actions. They have changed how they talk to students and treat students with more respect. - Teachers say students feel like they can be honest and express themselves better, and students feel less ashamed—maybe students feel this way because of this change in treatment. - One teacher says separating behavior from the student is important, so students don't feel like they're being labeled. This is key for reaching students with TNR language. - Teachers again emphasized the need for posters in Spanish.

continued →

Themes From Teacher Interviews	Synthesized Statements From Teachers
Student engagement	- Many teachers know that student engagement doesn't have to involve friendship—just mutual respect. According to one teacher, younger students (sixth and seventh graders) are more receptive to TNR language than eighth graders. - It's hard to engage students when teachers feel drained or burned out, and navigating quiet or uninterested students is a challenge. Teachers know that encouraging student engagement requires quality one-on-ones, reflection, and careful wording of what they say to students (for example, not making condescending comments or using blame and shame). - Teachers encourage students to do what they must do to be assertive for learning (for example, getting up and moving around). They give students time to be silly and let them know when it is time to be assertive.
Teacher self-reflection and emotions	- Teachers report a wide variety of self-reflections and emotions. Some reflect on their inadequacies with teaching methods and how lack of effort is discouraging even if student behavior is fine. - Teachers admit it's easier to focus on students who are making efforts to be engaged, and they still care for students who don't—they just want them to try. - One teacher feels "corny" using some of the TNR words. Some teachers report a more enjoyable classroom experience, less stress, and a better ability to be straightforward with students because of TNR, and that TNR allows them to understand what it means to respect and form real connections with students.
Changes in school culture	- There is a difference of opinions about school culture, regarding overall outlook and TNR involvement. Teachers credit TNR with better teacher conversations, collaborations, and empowering both students and teachers in the classroom. - Not everyone is on board with TNR, and teachers say that students know the difference between teachers who do and do not participate in TNR. Non-TNR teachers are more demanding and dictator-like, according to some teachers. - Teachers who use TNR appear to be like-minded in the sense that they love the improved classroom culture and camaraderie among staff, and embrace that it is a mindset and philosophy that supports students and even improves teacher behavior.

TABLE A.5: Student Focus-Group Interviews

Themes From Student Focus-Group Interviews	Synthesized Statements From Students
How my teachers use TNR language	• Teachers use the language to ask students to self-evaluate and identify their behaviors as they relate to their actions and schoolwork progress. • Teachers encourage honesty, and students say that the language helps them get back on track. • Students know that teachers use the language in a way that doesn't demean them but rather as a check-up on their behavior.
Self-assessment of behaviors (behaviors that got in the way)	• Many students identify being stuck, passive, shirking, and showboating. The online environment contributes to feelings of passive, silly, and stuck. • Students are aware of their behaviors, and the TNR language helps them recognize and explain these behaviors better. • Students feel more comfortable about speaking out when stuck, and they feel more obligated to get help when teachers are asking them about TNR language. • The TNR words act like a reminder for students to think about their actions.
Self-regulation of behaviors (how I changed my behaviors)	• Students self-regulate their behaviors by catching themselves or being told to self-evaluate, which makes them think about their actions and how that affects their work. One student mentions setting reminders to redirect them from distractions. • Teachers asking them to self-regulate with the TNR language helps them assess their intent with their actions and behaviors. • Teachers addressing the whole class about behaviors instead of singling out one student helps students reflect on their own behaviors.
How have I changed in terms of being a worker? (work ethic)	• Students report an overall improvement in their work ethic. Students work harder, get their assignments done, challenge themselves in the classroom, and understand how to get back on track.
How does TNR help me at school?	• The TNR language guides students toward getting work done in school. Students feel like they want to try harder and do better when they use that language. Merely saying "do your work" doesn't convey the same sentiments that the TNR language does. • Students say the language helps them focus (and refocus), get their work done quicker, makes it easier to ask for help and put more effort into their work.

continued →

Themes From Student Focus-Group Interviews	Synthesized Statements From Students
Do I use TNR outside of school?	• Students do use TNR outside of school! Some use it subconsciously, where they self-assess what they're doing and get back to their tasks. Some students use it in the family setting. One student thought about TNR while playing on a sports team.
Difference between TNR and non-TNR teachers	• Teachers who use TNR language can keep their students on track with assignments and get them to work harder. • Students say the language is more sympathetic and caring, compared to being asked, "Can you stop messing around?" or "Do your work." • Teachers using the language help validate how students feel and lets them know that they can reach out for help if needed. • Students say non-TNR teachers aren't as approachable as TNR teachers when asking for help. The TNR language motivates them to reflect and change their behaviors or actions accordingly.
Ways to improve TNR	• To improve TNR, students recommend that more teachers (in terms of number and subjects) use the TNR language and bring up TNR more often. • Teachers should also believe that TNR will work because students will believe it too. • Some students say to add more words and diversify the language to include students who don't understand TNR words.

What the Data Tell Us

So, what do the data tell us about using Tools Not Rules? What do they tell us about its successes and failures? What did we learn from this study, and how did it help us improve and refine the approach? Let's revisit our two research questions.

1. Does Tools Not Rules help create a safe, collaborative, and supportive learning environment for students?
2. Does Tools Not Rules help students develop their self-assessment and self-regulation skills?

Does Tools Not Rules Help Create a Safe, Collaborative, and Supportive Learning Environment for Students?

We felt encouraged and often surprised by the impact of using TNR during a year in which students started school fully online for the first few months. During the 2020–21 school year, students in the study returned to school when the COVID-19 numbers allowed moving back and forth between face-to-face and online instruction.

ADMINISTRATORS

Through all this unexpected and unprecedented educational upheaval, administrators felt that Tools Not Rules was creating stronger teacher-student connections, which created a supportive learning environment. One administrator mentioned in the interview that "TNR is having a really positive effect on new teachers coming to the middle school" because they can adopt it into their classrooms with greater effectiveness in teaching.

Another administrator mentioned that "Tools Not Rules teachers are thriving because they are not dealing with so much discipline in the classroom." And yet another administrator mentioned that they "love watching the language take all the negative energy out of a situation." Another shared that when using the TNR language, teachers are not fighting with students. Instead, "students are doing their own kind of self-reflection, and that has allowed teachers to feel like they are teaching kids, not managing them."

TEACHERS

Teachers in the study reported that Tools Not Rules allows for better conversations and collaboration with each other. They reflected that they sense a difference in classroom climate between teachers using TNR and those who are not. Teachers drawn to Tools Not Rules may be like-minded and feel a kinship in this type of work with students, enjoying the improved behavior, culture, and camaraderie among the staff. Teachers in the study felt TNR empowers both students and teachers to make positive changes in their behaviors.

Based on the pre- and post-survey results, there are several interesting data points to consider. Teachers using Tools Not Rules had a 16.56 percent positive change in their belief that the school is developing their capacity for positive connections between students and staff. By the end of the year, non-TNR teachers dropped 7.19 percent in their perception of this same statement. Similarly, when reflecting on collaboration about how to effectively engage students, TNR teachers increased

28.38 percent, while non-TNR teachers dropped 2.91 percent. One measure that underscored the use of Tools Not Rules in the classroom was expecting honesty. TNR teachers increased by 16.12 percent, while non-TNR teachers decreased by 5.95 percent.

These results indicate that using Tools Not Rules in the classroom helps create a collaborative, supportive, and safe learning environment for students and teachers. It appears to increase collaboration among teachers about how to help students while also improving honest conversations. As one teacher shared, "TNR gives me tools for honesty. Students are more open and honest about what is really going on."

Does Tools Not Rules Help Students Develop Their Self-Assessment and Self-Regulation Skills?

During the student focus-group interviews, students reported that TNR encouraged them to think about what they were doing and why they might be doing it. Students also responded to teachers who used the language and often interpreted this as the teacher asking them what they needed and reminding them to ask for help.

One student shared: "My writing wasn't that good, but now when I'm using the TNR words, I think I got better." This student shared that she never asked questions in class about her writing, even though she knew she was struggling. As a multilingual student, she felt embarrassed and didn't want to disappoint her teacher. When her teacher used Tools Not Rules, she felt that asking for help was expected, and her teacher invited her to do so every day. This is what she meant by "using the TNR words." I wanted to know if this student applied the language outside the classroom, and she said, "Yeah, I think about it all the time. When my mom asked me to do things to help her, I realized I was being passive when I just sat on my phone and ignored her. I didn't want to be passive, so I got up and started doing things." When I asked if her relationship with her mom had changed, she smiled and replied, "Yeah, it's a lot better."

Another student shared: "Instead of being passive and doing nothing, I would actually get work done—and that's something I'm proud of because I'm starting to do more work, I'm able to learn more, and I'm getting good grades." Another student shared, "I feel more motivated to work harder when we use that language because I don't want to be like, 'Oh, I'm being passive, or I'm stuck.' I feel like I try harder when we use that language."

Each of these statements demonstrates self-assessment and self-regulation, and employing Tools Not Rules triggers these actions. Students have pride in their work and recognize their autonomy in making this happen. When used as intended, students seem to interpret the TNR language and approach as a call to improve themselves under the most caring conditions. As one eighth grader mentioned in the interview, "Changing who you are on the inside is a lot harder than just changing and building on what's already there. It's hard to build off nothing. Once you have that foundation that you've built . . . you can always change going upward and forward." Upward and forward equals hope, confidence, and resilience. We all want this for students, and Tools Not Rules has the right ingredients to create the classroom conditions under which it can flourish and grow.

Conclusion

Based on these study results and our experience using Tools Not Rules with students, we'd like to think that TNR has solutions for students and teachers who feel disconnected, anxious, alone, and frustrated in the classroom. The study results show that TNR can increase student and teacher autonomy, belongingness, and connection. TNR offers a chance for you to react with curiosity (instead of judgment) as a first step when working with student behavior. Students don't expect teachers to be curious about their behavior—instead, they expect anger, shame, and maybe a lecture. Students can build up a stubborn shield against this type of transactional relationship.

But curiosity is different, and it confuses them. They stop and look at you as if to say, "This is not how the conversation is supposed to go!" In this moment, you have created an opportunity for a real and relevant teacher-student connection. It transforms you from manager to teacher. It allows you to be warm ("I understand what you are saying, and I'm going to help you by . . . ") and demanding ("Tell me what you are going to do right now to get started"). The Tools Not Rules approach can help both teachers and students become happier and increasingly successful, confident in the ability to go upward and forward!

In retrospect, spending the pandemic year focusing on Tools Not Rules students, and teaching was an amazing privilege. Meeting each week was a constant in the chaos of the pandemic—it allowed everyone a space for potential, positivity, and hope to flourish. Many teachers who participated in the study still use TNR; some have moved to different districts; a few have taken administrative positions; and several still teach at the same middle school. As a continuation of our work in the middle school where we conducted the study, we are meeting with new teachers (and anyone else who would like to join) to focus on specific student behaviors that challenge us and how we can leverage Tools Not Rules to help. This work continues to teach us the value of Tools Not Rules for educators, especially those starting their careers in the post-pandemic classroom.

References and Resources

Armitage, J. M., Collishaw, S., & Sellers, R. (2024). Explaining long-term trends in adolescent emotional problems: What we know from population-based studies. *Discover Social Science and Health*, *4*(1), 14–17. https://doi.org/10.1007/s44155-024-00076-2

Bandura, A. (1977). *Social learning theory*. Englewood Cliffs, NJ: Prentice Hall.

Bertolone-Smith, C., Puliatte, A., Dale, S., Unigarro, M., & Vantassel, D. (2023). What pre-service teachers want math to know: Examining self-identified relationships and critical experiences with mathematics. *Excelsior: Leadership in Teaching and Learning*, *15*(2), 193–213. https://doi.org/10.14305/jn.19440413.2023.15.2.05

Bornstein, J. (2017). Can PBIS build justice rather than merely restore order? In N. Okilwa & M. Khalifa (Eds.), *The school to prison pipeline: The role of culture and discipline in school* (Vol. 4; pp. 135–167). Emerald Publishing Limited. https://doi.org/10.1108/S2051-231720160000004008

Brown, B. (2011, December). *The power of vulnerability* [Video]. TED. Accessed at www.youtube.com/watch?v=iCvmsMzlF7ohttps://www.ted.com/talks/brene_brown_listening_to_shame?language=en on August 23, 2023.

Brown, B. (2012a). *Daring greatly: How the courage to be vulnerable transform the way we live, love, parent, and lead*. New York: Penguin Random House.

Brown, B. (2012b, March). *Listening to shame* [Video]. Accessed at www.ted.com/talks/brene_brown_listening_to_shame?language=en on September 22, 2023.

Brown, B. (2021). *Atlas of the heart*. New York: Penguin Random House.

CASEL. (n.d.). *What is the CASEL framework?* Accessed at https://casel.org/fundamentals-of-sel/what-is-the-casel-framework/#self-management on November 22, 2023.

Data USA. (n.d.). *South Lake Tahoe, CA: Economy.* Accessed at https://datausa.io/profile/geo/south-lake-tahoe-ca?redirect=true#economy on November 22, 2023.

Douglas County School District. (n.d.). *EPIC learning.* Accessed at www.dcsd.net/about/epic on June 5, 2024.

Dweck, C. S. (2008). *Mindsets and math/science achievement report.* Accessed at www.growthmindsetmaths.com/uploads/2/3/7/7/23776169/mindset_and_math_science_achievement_-_nov_2013.pdf on September 22, 2023.

Dweck, C. S. (2015, December 15). *RSA animate: How to help every child fulfill their potential* [Video]. Accessed at www.youtube.com/watch?v=Yl9TVbAal5s on September 30, 2024.

Dweck, C. S. (2016). *Mindset: The new psychology of success* (Updated ed.). New York: Random House.

Frankl, V. (1959). *Man's search for meaning.* Boston: Beacon Press.

Gibbs, P. (1996). *What is Occam's Razor?* Accessed at https://math.ucr.edu/home/baez/physics/General/occam.html on September 9, 2023.

Ginwright, S. A. (2022). *The four pivots: Reimagining justice, reimagining ourselves.* Berkeley, CA: North Atlantic Books.

Hammond, Z. (2014). *Culturally responsive teaching and the brain: Promoting authentic engagement and rigor among culturally and linguistically diverse students.* Thousand Oaks, CA: Corwin.

Harvard University Center on the Developing Child. (n.d.). *How to motivate children: Science-based approaches for parents, caregivers, and teachers.* Accessed at https://developingchild.harvard.edu/resources/how-to-motivate-children-science-based-approaches-for-parents-caregivers-and-teachers on September 30, 2024.

Hattie, J. (2009). *Visible learning: A synthesis of over 800 meta-analyses relating to achievement.* London: Routledge.

Hattie, J. (2023). *Visible learning: The sequel—A synthesis of over 2,100 meta-analyses relating to achievement.* London: Routledge.

Heflebower, T., Hoegh, J. K., Warrick, P. B., & Flygare, J. (2018). *A teacher's guide to standards-based learning: An instruction manual for adopting standards-based grading, curriculum, and feedback* (1st ed.). Denver, CO: Marzano Resources.

Hoge, E., Bickham, D., & Cantor, J. (2017). Digital media, anxiety, and depression in children. *Pediatrics Issue Supplement, 2*(140), S76–S80. https://doi.org/10.1542/peds.2016-1758G

Jensen, E. (2019). *Poor students, rich teaching: Seven high-impact mindsets for students from poverty (Using mindsets in the classroom to overcome student poverty and adversity).* Bloomington, IN: Solution Tree Press.

KidsData. (2024). *All data: Lake Tahoe Unified.* Accessed at www.kidsdata.org/region/426/lake-tahoe-unified/results#ind=&say=&cat=6,18 on June 13, 2024.

Knopf, A. (2021). Adverse mental health effects of COVID-19 on children and teens. *The Brown University Child and Adolescent Psychopharmacology Update, 23*(5), 7. https://doi.org/10.1002/cpu.30577

Langer-Osuna, J. M. (2017). Authority, identity, and collaborative mathematics. *Journal for Research in Mathematics Education, 48*(3), 237–247. https://doi.org/10.5951/jresematheduc.48.3.0237

Liljedahl, P. (2021). *Building thinking classrooms in mathematics, grades K–12: 14 teaching practices for enhancing learning* (1st ed.). Thousand Oaks, CA: Corwin.

Marzano, R. (2017). *The new art and science of teaching.* Denver, CO: Marzano Resources.

Marzano, R., Rains, C., & Warrick, P. (2020). *Improving teacher development and evaluation.* Bloomington, IN: Marzano Resources.

Marzano, R., Warrick, P. B., Rains, C. L., & DuFour, R. (2018). *Leading a high reliability school.* Bloomington, IN: Solution Tree Press.

Marzano Resources. (n.d.). *Marzano high reliability schools.* Accessed at www.marzanoresources.com/hrs/high-reliability-schools#conIframewrapp on November 22, 2023.

Maslow, A. H. (1943). A theory of human motivation. *Psychological Review, 50*(4), 370–396. https://doi.org/10.1037/h0054346

McLeod, S. (2023). *Maslow's hierarchy of needs.* Accessed at www.simplypsychology.org/maslow.html on July 15, 2022.

Reyes, M. R., Brackett, M. A., Rivers, S. E., White, M., & Salovey, P. (2012). Classroom emotional climate, student engagement, and academic achievement. *Journal of Educational Psychology, 104*(3), 700–712. https://doi.org/10.1037/a0027268

Romero, V., Robertson, R., & Warner, A. (2018). *Building resilience in students impacted by adverse childhood experiences: A whole-staff approach.* Thousand Oaks, CA: Corwin.

Rose, J., & Steen, S. (2014). The achieving success everyday group counseling model: Fostering resiliency in middle school students. *Professional School Counseling, 18*(1). https://doi.org/10.1177/2156759X0001800116

Saban, N. (2023). *What Nick Saban said at 2023 SEC Media Days.* Accessed at www.youtube.com/watch?v=X476lxAxDCo on October 15, 2023.

Scanfeld, V., Davis, L., Weintraub, L., & Dotoli, V. (2018). The power of common language. *Educational Leadership, 76*(1), 54–58. Accessed at www.ascd.org/el/articles/the-power-of-common-language on August 30, 2023.

Siegel, D., & Bryson, T. P. (2020). *The power of showing up.* New York: Ballantine Books.

Silverstein, S. (1978). "INVITATION (Where the sidewalk ends)." In *Where the sidewalk ends.* New York: HarperCollins Children's Books.

Sommers, S., Unigarro, M., Vantassel, D., Bertolone-Smith, C., & Puliatte, A. (2022) Draw a picture of yourself learning math: What pre-service teachers' self-portraits illustrate about their complex relationships with mathematics. *Journal on Empowering Teaching Excellence, 6*(1), Article 3. Accessed at https://digitalcommons.usu.edu/jete/vol6/iss1/3 on June 3, 2024.

Suspensions and expulsions: willful defiance: interventions and supports (2023). *California Senate Bill 274.* Accessed at https://legiscan.com/CA/text/SB274/id/2832497 on January 9, 2023.

Swaak, T. (2019, September 18). *As California expands ban on 'willful defiance' suspensions, lessons from L.A. schools, which barred them six years ago.* Accessed at www.the74million.org/article/as-california-expands-ban-on-willful-defiance-suspensions-lessons-from-l-a-schools-which-barred-them-six-years-ago on November 1, 2023.

Twenge, J. M. (2017). *Gen: Why today's super-connected kids are growing up less rebellious, more tolerant, less happy—and completely unprepared for adulthood and (what this means for the rest of us).* New York: Atria.

Twenge, J. M., Haidt, J., Joiner, T. E., & Campbell, W. K. (2020). Underestimating digital media harm. *Nature Human Behavior, 4,* 346–348. https://doi.org/10.1038/s41562-020-0839-4

U.S. News. (2024). *South Tahoe Middle.* Accessed at www.usnews.com/education/k12/california/south-tahoe-middle-268534 on June 13, 2024.

Van Der Kolk, B. (2014) *The body keeps the score: Brain, mind, and body in the healing of trauma.* New York: Viking Press.

Wolcott, G. (2019). *Significant 72: Unleashing the power of relationships in today's schools.* Oshkosh, WI: FIRST Educational Resources.

Wood, M. B. (2013). Mathematical micro-identities: Moment-to-moment positioning and learning in a fourth-grade classroom. *Journal for Research in Mathematics Education, 44*(5), 775–808. https://doi.org/10.5951/jresematheduc.44.5.0775

Wortham, S. (2008). From good student to outcast: The emergence of a classroom identity. *Ethos, 32,* 164–187. https://doi.org/10.1525/eth.2004.32.2.164

Index

A

accountability
    honesty and, 19, 28–29, 33
    relationships and, 42
    scenarios for, 43, 44, 45, 46
    TNR, principles of, 7
administrator interviews, 142
adopting the TNR language. *See also* TNR language
    about, 51–52
    common language and, 57–58
    conclusion, 65
    engagement, increasing, 62–65
    logic behind the three triads, 56–57
    meaning of TNR language, 52–56
    predictable approaches, value of, 59–61
    student story for, 58–59
    TNR language to support schoolwide programs, 61–62
    try this, 66
adverse childhood experiences (ACEs), 47, 111
assessment, individual and group assessment, 88, 91–93. *See also* self-assessment

B

behavior. *See also* identity and behavior
    behavioral output, 38
    different approach to, 36–41
    growth mindsets and, 39–40
    TNR, principles of, 7
    TNR and handling challenging behavior, 126–127
Bertolone-Smith, C., Claudia's journey, 2–3
Brown, B., 21, 26, 27, 28, 31, 40
Building Resilience in Students Impacted by Adverse Childhood Experiences: A Whole-Staff Approach (Romero, Robertson, and Warner), 55–56
Building Thinking Classrooms in Mathematics, Grades K-12: 14 Teaching Practices for Enhancing Learning (Liljedhal), 56

C

changing the most challenging behavior with star chart. *See* star charts
charades, 74
classroom meetings and circles, 49
classroom routines, establishing, 114–116
Collaborative for Academic, Social, and Emotional Learning (CASEL), 132
communessential, use of term, 125
connection oriented scenario. *See* relationships
connection oriented scenarios, 43, 44, 45, 46
conversations, setting parameters for individual student conversations, 111–112

D

describing what it looks like, 74–75
disconnection oriented scenarios, 43–44, 44–45, 46
disengagement, 60
dysregulation, 55

E

engagement
    engagement strategies, 63–65
    increased engagement and the TNR language, 62–65
    Magic, Fuzzy Numbers and, 86
    Marzano's highly effective teaching actions and, 32
ensuring honesty above all else. *See* honesty
environmental input, 38
EPIC (Empower, Prepare, Inspire, Connect) Learning, 61
establishing that you are not your behavior. *See* identity and behavior
expectations, 31, 32, 42, 43
eyes and hands strategy, 63–64. *See also* engagement

F

fixed mindsets, 29–30. *See also* growth mindsets
flexible mindsets, 30. *See also* growth mindsets
Four Pivots: Reimagining Justice, Reimagining Ourselves, The (Ginwright), 112
Frankl, V., 38

G

gifted students, 30–31
Ginwright, S., 112
give me twenty-five strategy, 64–65. *See also* engagement
growth mindsets, 30, 39–40, 83

H

Hammond, Z., 41
highly effective teacher actions, 31–32
honesty
    about, 17–18
    accountability and, 28–29
    conclusion, 33
    example poster for, 18
    as the foundation, 18–19, 21
    honest conversations, 21, 22, 26–27
    scenarios for, 19–21, 22–25
    student story for, 27–28
    TNR, principles of, 7
    TNR for all students, striving and advanced, 29–32
    TNR language, lesson sequence for rolling out, 79
    try this, 33

I

identity and behavior
    about, 35–36
    conclusion, 50
    different approach to behavior, 36–41
    positive student-teacher relationships and, 41–46
    student story for, 48–49
    students are watching/student observations of teachers, 47–50
    TNR language, lesson sequence for rolling out, 79
    try this, 50
interventions, model of TNR conversations and interventions for students, 22
introduction
    about this book, 14–16
    Claudia's journey, 2–3
    conclusion, 16
    how an idea became Tools Not Rules, 5–6
    Marlene's journey, 3–5
    TNR, principles of, 7, 12–13
    TNR study, 13–14
"Invitation" (Silverstein), 125

L

labels/labeling, 33, 37–38, 143
language triads. *See also* Tools Not Rules (TNR)
    example for TNR word triads, 53–54
    how an idea became Tools Not Rules, 5–6
    logic behind, 56–57

Index

meaning of TNR language, 52–56
this book and, 14
learning environments
    highly effective teaching actions and, 32
    TNR and, 13–14, 61, 127, 147–148
lifting our learning and activities for teaching TNR language, 76
Liljedhal, P., 56

M

macro-identities, 37. *See also* identity and behavior
Magic, Fuzzy Numbers, 83–86, 87
Marzano, R., 61
mediational processes, 38
modeling redirection, 76–78
moving forward
    community of educators and, 128
    confidence and handling challenging behaviors, 126–127
    courage and creating the classroom you and your students deserve, 127
    invitation to, 125–126
    personal experiences and, 129
Moyer, M., Marlene's journey, 3–5
multitiered systems of support (MTSS), 132

N

New Art and Science of Teaching, The (Marzano), 61
normalizing, 27
norms, establishing, 114–116

O

Occam's razor, 104
overcoming implementation challenges and realizing possibilities. *See also* Tools Not Rules (TNR)
    about, 107–108
    challenges, 108–112
    conclusion, 122
    possibilities, 112–116
    student perception surveys, 116–122
    try this, 122–123

P

passive, assertive, aggressive. *See also* language triads
    actions, not labels and, 37
    example for TNR word triads, 54
    how an idea became Tools Not Rules, 5
    lesson sequence for rolling out TNR language, 80, 81–82
    logic behind the three triads, 56
    making TNR words fit every classroom, 109, 110
    meaning of TNR language, 52, 54, 55
positive behavioral interventions and supports (PBIS), 47, 61, 62, 132
praising students, new way, 83–88

R

redirection, modeling, 76–78
relationships
    connection oriented scenarios, 43, 44, 45, 46
    highly effective teaching actions and, 32
    honesty and, 21
    impact of, 31–32, 49
    positive student-teacher relationships, 41–46
    setting parameters for individual student conversations, 112
    shame and, 40
    social-emotional learning, five areas of, 132
reluctant learners, 26
resilience, 27, 132
responsible decision making, 132
restorative justice, 62, 132
Roberston, R., 55–56
Romero, V., 55–56
Rose, J., 132
rules and procedures, TNR and highly effective actions and, 32

S

Saban, N., 42
self-assessment
    individual conversations and, 111
    individual self-assessment, 88, 91–92

language triads and, 14
scenarios for, 89–90, 91
social-emotional learning, five areas
    of, 133
student story for, 48–49
student-focused group interviews, 145
TNR, principles of, 7, 12, 42,
    132–133
TNR for all students, 29, 31
TNR language and, 68, 70
TNR study and, 148–149
whole-group self-assessment, 92–93
self-awareness, 56, 132, 133
self-management, 28, 62, 132, 133
self-regulation
    honesty and, 18
    individual conversations and, 111
    language triads and, 14
    student story for, 48–49
    student-focused group interviews
        and, 145
    TNR, principles of, 7, 12, 42,
        132–133
    TNR for all students, 29, 31
    TNR language and, 68, 70, 108, 110
    TNR study and, 148–149
setting the standard and activities for
    teaching TNR language, 78
shirking, working, showboating. See also
    language triads
    actions, not labels and, 37
    example for TNR word triads, 53
    how an idea became Tools Not Rules, 5
    lesson sequence for rolling out TNR
        language, 80, 81–82
    making TNR words fit every
        classroom, 109, 110
    meaning of TNR language, 52, 54, 55
*Significant 72: Unleashing the Power of
    Relationships in Today's Schools* (Wolcott), 7
Silverstein, S., 125
social awareness, 132
social learning theory, 38
social-emotional learning, five areas of, 132
stalemates, 39–40
standards and activities for teaching TNR
    language, 78
star charts
    about, 95–96

benefits of, 101–113
conclusion, 105
effectiveness of, 104–105
examples of, 96, 98
how to use, 99–103
privacy and, 100–101
rewards and, 100
star chart story, 96–99
supports and reinforcements for,
    103–104
try this, 105
Steen, S., 132
stories, sharing, 74
stress
    reducing teacher stress, 112–114
    technology and, 133
    TNR language and, 54
striving students, 29–32
stuck, serious, silly. See also language triads
    actions, not labels and, 37
    example for TNR word triads, 53
    how an idea became Tools Not Rules, 5
    lesson sequence for rolling out TNR
        language, 79, 80, 81–82
    logic behind the three triads, 56
    making TNR words fit every
        classroom, 109
    meaning of TNR language, 52, 54, 55
student conversations, setting parameters for,
    111–112
student perception surveys. See also surveys
    about, 116–119
    example of, 117–118
    low scores, meaning behind, 120–121
    obtaining significant insights, 119–120
    personal issues, identifying and
        attending, 121–122
students
    identifying and attending to students'
        personal issues, 121–122
    student well-being, increasing, 114
    student-focused group interviews,
        145–146
    students are watching/student
        observations of teachers, 47–50
    student-teacher relationships. See
        relationships
    TNR for all students, striving and
        advanced, 29–32

surveys. *See also* student perception surveys
    pre and post school survey results, 138–139
    school climate survey, 136–137
    student perception surveys, 116–122
suspensions, 39, 45, 62, 104

T

teachers
    highly effective teacher actions, 31–32
    reducing teacher stress, 112–114
    teacher interviews, 143–144
    teacher-student relationships. *See* relationships
teaching and using the TNR language with students. *See also* TNR language
    about, 67–68
    conclusion, 93–94
    how to teach students the TNR language, 68–74
    individual and group assessment, 88, 91–93
    praising students, new way for, 83–88
    rolling out the TNR language, plan for, 78–82
    scenarios for, 71–72, 89–90, 91, 92
    setting the stage, 71
    simple activities for teaching TNR language, 74–78
    try this, 94
    we, importance of, 72–74
TNR language. *See also* adopting the TNR language; language triads; teaching and using the TNR language with students; Tools Not Rules (TNR)
    getting started with, 108
    how to teach students, 68–74
    making TNR words fit every classroom, 108–111
    meaning of, 52–56
    rolling out the TNR language, plan for, 78–82
    simple activities for teaching, 74–78
    to support schoolwide programs, 61–62
TNR study. *See also* Tools Not Rules (TNR)
    about, 13–14, 131
    administrator interviews, 142
    conclusion, 149
    data analysis and, 138, 140–141
    participating teacher interviews, 143–144
    percentage change on selected statements comparing teachers who participated in the TNR training and those who did not, 140–141
    pre and post school survey results, 138–139
    school climate survey, 136–137
    school demographics and study participants, 133–135
    student focus-group interviews, 145–146
    study background, 131–133
    what the data tells us, 146–149
Tools Not Rules (TNR). *See also* overcoming implementation challenges and realizing possibilities; TNR language; TNR study
    for all students, striving and advanced, 29–32
    development of, 4
    ensuring honesty above all else. *See* honesty
    example of posters for the classroom, 8, 69–70, 109
    highly effective teaching actions and, 32
    how an idea became, 5–6
    model of TNR conversations and interventions for students, 22
    personal experiences with, 129
    principles of, 7, 12–13
    scenario for, 8–12
    TNR rationale scenario, 43, 44, 45, 46
trauma, 111, 115

V

vulnerability, 21

W

warm demanders, 41
Warner, A., 55–56
well-being, increasing student, 114
what it looks like and activities for teaching TNR language, 74–75
Wolcott, G., 7, 40

Teaching Self-Regulation
Amy S. Gaumer Erickson and Patricia M. Noona
Self-regulation fuels students to become socially and emotionally engaged, lifelong learners. With this timely resource, you'll gain 75 instructional activities to teach self-regulation in any secondary classroom. Ample teacher-tested tools and templates are also included to help you create authentic learning experiences and deliver effective feedback.
BKF988

Motivated to Learn
Staci M. Zolkoski, Calli Lewis Chiu, and Mandy E. Lusk
In *Motivated to Learn*, you will gain evidence-based approaches for engaging students and equipping them to better focus in the classroom. With this book's straightforward strategies, you can learn to motivate all your students to actively participate in learning.
BKG037

The Metacognitive Student
Richard K. Cohen, Deanne Kildare Opatosky, James Savage, Susan Olsen Stevens, and Edward P. Darrah
What if there was one strategy you could use to support students academically, socially, and emotionally? It exists—and it's simple, straightforward, and practical. Dive deep into structured SELf-questioning and learn how to empower students to develop into strong, healthy, and confident thinkers.
BKF954

Brick by Brick
Kjell Fenn
Using research-supported strategies, author Kjell Fenn guides new teachers through four pillars of successful teaching: planning, structure, engagement, and confidence. Learn how to design assessments, craft lesson plans, and find the structure for students and teachers to experience joy in the classroom.
BKG214

Solution Tree | Press

Visit SolutionTree.com or call 800.733.6786 to order.

Wait! Your professional development journey doesn't have to end with the last pages of this book.

We realize improving student learning doesn't happen overnight. And your school or district shouldn't be left to puzzle out all the details of this process alone.

No matter where you are on the journey, we're committed to helping you get to the next stage.

Take advantage of everything from **custom workshops** to **keynote presentations** and **interactive web and video conferencing**. We can even help you develop an action plan tailored to fit your specific needs.

Let's get the conversation started.

Call 888.763.9045 today.

SolutionTree.com